ROUTLEDGE LIBRARY EDITIONS:
RENAISSANCE DRAMA

Volume 14

SHAKESPEARE'S TRAGIC JUSTICE

SHAKESPEARE'S TRAGIC JUSTICE

C. J. SISSON

LONDON AND NEW YORK

First published in 1963 by Methuen & Co Ltd

This edition first published in 2017
by Routledge
2 Park Square, Milton Park, Abingdon, Oxon OX14 4RN

and by Routledge
711 Third Avenue, New York, NY 10017

Routledge is an imprint of the Taylor & Francis Group, an informa business

© 1963 C. J. Sisson

All rights reserved. No part of this book may be reprinted or reproduced or utilised in any form or by any electronic, mechanical, or other means, now known or hereafter invented, including photocopying and recording, or in any information storage or retrieval system, without permission in writing from the publishers.

Trademark notice: Product or corporate names may be trademarks or registered trademarks, and are used only for identification and explanation without intent to infringe.

British Library Cataloguing in Publication Data
A catalogue record for this book is available from the British Library

ISBN: 978-1-138-71372-7 (Set)
ISBN: 978-1-315-19807-1 (Set) (ebk)
ISBN: 978-1-138-23462-8 (Volume 14) (hbk)
ISBN: 978-1-138-23465-9 (Volume 14) (pbk)
ISBN: 978-1-315-30639-1 (Volume 14) (ebk)

Publisher's Note
The publisher has gone to great lengths to ensure the quality of this reprint but points out that some imperfections in the original copies may be apparent.

Disclaimer
The publisher has made every effort to trace copyright holders and would welcome correspondence from those they have been unable to trace.

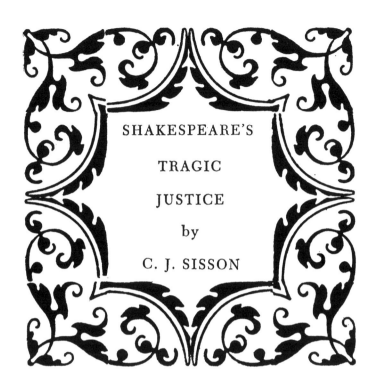

SHAKESPEARE'S TRAGIC JUSTICE

by

C. J. SISSON

METHUEN & CO LTD

36 ESSEX STREET, LONDON WC2

2/2549/10

*All rights reserved
Printed and bound
in Canada
by W. J. Gage Limited*

Designed by Arnold Rockman MTDC

Introduction, 1

I
Public justice: Macbeth, 11

II
Private justice: Othello, 28

III
The dilemma: Hamlet, 52

IV
The quandary: King Lear, 74

Appendix on Hamlet, 99

PREFACE

Justice is an intensely alive problem in the world of today, affecting alike the individual in the conduct of his own life, the State in its organisation of society and its administration of the law, and the inter-relations of States and communities. It was a matter of no less deep concern to Elizabethan England.

Attempts have been made of late to increase Shakespeare's stature, or perhaps to make him more palatable to contemporary taste, by reading into his plays significances of moment mainly or exclusively for our own day, even in the form of concepts that were literally unthinkable to Shakespeare and his day, such as the notorious Oedipus Complex as the basic theme of *Hamlet*. It is not thus that Shakespeare is vindicated as 'for all time'. In his plays he reflects his own thought, and the life and thought of his own time, and in so doing presents dramatic pictures of problems of life that are significant to all ages of mankind. By virtue of his deep humanity and creative imaginativeness Shakespeare is both 'of an age' and 'for all time'.

The problem of justice, human and divine, seems to have haunted Shakespeare, as it haunted Renaissance Christendom, and as it emerges most plainly in his greatest tragedies. Of these four studies of justice in action, that of *King Lear* may well appear, if understood aright, to have gone far beyond the most advanced present-day thought on this most poignant problem of life and society. Here indeed it is not for us to seek to bring Shakespeare level with us today, but to raise ourselves to his level.

INTRODUCTION

It is generally held that Shakespeare's last plays reflect a turning in his later years to a more benign observation of life and character, in which a warm optimism colours his representation of human nature. 'Some shall be pardoned and some punished' is the judgment of the Prince at the end of *Romeo and Juliet,* an early tragedy. But 'Pardon's the word to all' in *Cymbeline,* freeing even Iachimo, the plotter of evil, whose penitence is sharply contrasted with the obduracy of Iago in *Othello.* Justice, it might seem, is increasingly superseded by mercy in the dramatic world over which Shakespeare ruled.

Comedy, of course, has a logic of its own that differs from the logic of tragedy, and Shakespeare's latest plays are comedies, though *Cymbeline* happens to be included among the *Tragedies* in the First Folio. It is noticeable that the most powerful and moving appeals to mercy occur in an early comedy, *The Merchant of Venice,* and in a late comedy, *Measure for Measure.* And it is perhaps significant that in each instance the appeal comes from a woman, from Portia and from Isabella. Isabella's plea, indeed, interprets for us the deep-laid foundations of Elizabethan thought upon justice and mercy. Mercy must temper justice in human society if the world of men is to resemble the spiritual world of which it seeks to be the faint and imperfect image. Under the justice of God all men stand condemned for sin, and their sole hope lies in His mercy, which is infinite. Shakespeare was born and lived in an atmosphere of thought in which human justice reflected this conception of divine justice. His father and his father-in-law alike, in offending against the laws of the manors of which they were tenants, had come to stand, in the immemorial phrase, in the mercy of the Lord of a Manor. The prerogative of mercy lay in the powers of a King, the fountain of justice, God's representative on earth, and from him the laws ultimately derived, though he delegated their administration.

Under the Tudors, however, that delegation was far from complete in the great Prerogative Courts, which were closely linked up with the King's Privy Council. In these courts the reserved power of the fountain of justice made itself felt against the operation of common law and statute law, and they were of all-pervading significance in Shakespeare's England as Courts of Appeal against the Common Law Courts. The Court of Requests, a poor man's court, wrote Sir Francis Walsingham in 1583, is 'appointed to mitigate the rigour of proceeding at law.' Portia's appeal to Shylock for mercy and reconciliation would seem familiar ground to the judges in the Court of Chancery. It was their aim to bring opposing parties to agreement rather than to judgment, and even when judgment was given, and before a final decree was passed, to plead with the successful party to show mercy and pity, as we may read the records extant of their decrees and orders.

When Shakespeare died, a little more than midway through the reign of King James, a marked change was coming over the atmosphere of thought concerning justice. It is familiar in the views of the famous John Selden, a great Common Lawyer and historian of the law. For him the true basis of the law, as of the monarchy, is a social contract. 'A King is a thing men have made for their own sakes, for quietness' sake'.[1] The law is a body of rules, 'as we have agreed to do one to another by public agreement.' Law is therefore a safe standard to abide by, where 'equity is a roguish thing,'[2] uncertain and changeable. In such a view, justice descends to earth and renounces all divine sanction and exemplar for human society. Whatever the rights of this conflict in juristic theory—and it was one of the fundamental causes of the Civil War—it is clear that the older traditional conception was more fitted to the purposes of the drama and to the exposition of problems of justice in human life, linking them up with the infinities of moral and spiritual law, and presenting their arbiter as a Duke, a Prince, or a King.

Shylock, it might seem, would have had Selden's support against any mitigation by mercy of the rigours

1. *Table Talk*. Ed. Arber. p. 60.
2. *Ib.* p. 46.

of the common law. If a man loses his all by a bad bargain, so that his wife and children must starve, Selden's answer is merely 'let him look to the making of his bargain,'[1] the very echo in his *Table Talk* of Shylock's 'let him look to his bond.' Shylock is indeed a good Common Lawyer, and cannot find charity mentioned in his bond. But the drama must concern itself with the spirit of the law, not with the arid abstractions of the letter of the law.

There is little scope in the documentary debates of the common law for the display of those moral and spiritual conflicts which impassion men's minds and characters and which are the true material of drama. For their fullest display in Shakespeare we must turn to his tragedies. In them we see a powerful mind and imagination deeply concerned with problems of justice, especially in the four tragedies under consideration here, each of which presents Shakespeare's dramatic treatment of a crucial question.

The interpretation of Shakespeare's tragedies, indeed, can never with safety move far from the orbit of conceptions of justice, and there is great need for the clarification of prevailing conceptions upon which so much has been made to rest. It is evident, for example, that some notion of poetic justice has for long dominated the consideration of tragedy in general, indeed ever since Aristotle's classical treatment of Greek tragedy. It is no less clear that to justify this statement the phrase 'poetic justice' requires explanation. Like most phrases in common use in literary criticism, it is changeable taffeta.

The great *New English Dictionary* is not very help-

1. *Ib.* p. 65.

ful here. The only example cited is a late use by Pope signifying justice meted out *to* poetry, and not *by* poetry. For Walter Pater, in *Appreciations*, it means simply measure for measure, the *lex talionis* which we find allegorised in Spenser's *Faerie Queene* in the shape of Talus the Iron Man, Artegall's page, the flail of Justice. As you sow, so shall you reap. And the wages of sin is death. Poetic justice, in the sense of justice in its poetic application or exemplification, has recently led Professor Lily Campbell to the interpretation of Shakespeare's tragedies as moral *exempla,* parables, allegories of vices and virtues, sermons, cautionary tales. There, but for the grace of God, go you or I.

It is uncritical to allow ourselves to be guided by an instinctive revulsion against such an approach to the tragedies, by an intuitive certainty that all that is most significant in tragedy is bypassed in such a theory. But intuition is strengthened by conviction, it seems to me, when we consider how few mortals indeed, if any, are likely but for the grace of God to go the way of Hamlet or of Lear, to take extreme instances. It may perhaps be thought that *Antony and Cleopatra* comes nearer to men's hearts and bosoms, and offers a fair target to the preacher. But Shakespeare's Antony and Shakespeare's Cleopatra reduce to a derisive level the glossy affairs of Hollywood or the absorbing excitements of lesser people in daily life, charming as they may be in youth at least. We *have* no worlds to lose for love. There is a moral of a kind in this, but not one to be set forth from a pulpit. It is of the very essence of Shakespeare's greatest creations that they have that quality of uniqueness which unfits them for service as object lessons.

For Dryden, poetic justice meant the appropriate

punishment of wickedness, and this notion has developed into the more complex notion of punishment or reward which is *peculiarly* appropriate in the ideal world of creative fiction, as compared with the real world of statute-law, and which satisfies the niceness of aesthetic judgment. Wackford Squeers beaten with his own birch, Iago caught in the toils he laid for another, the engineer hoist with his own petard, Desdemona strangled in her own bed, the bed she has contaminated, these may exemplify the satisfactory irony of such poetic justice. 'The justice of it pleases,' said Othello. Poetic justice here is firmly linked with the ancient notions of decorum in art, of which it is one aspect. We should of course be hard put to it to apply such a notion to the fate of Desdemona in *Othello*. A handkerchief is mislaid, a fib is told, and Paradise is lost. There is no inevitability here, no proportion, and no pleasing irony. The handkerchief itself is an offence against decorum in high tragedy, according to the Tony Lumpkins who hate everything that's low, and who translate *kerchief* as *mouchoir*, with the ludicrous associations of this word in the French language. The root of the matter here is, however, that Desdemona's fate harmonizes with no definable concept of justice, and we have to face the fact.

Poetic justice in this narrow sense may perhaps be felt to be at work in the tangled events that comprise the catastrophe in *Hamlet*, but only in respect of the fall of Hamlet's antagonists, Claudius above all. But who would be entirely at ease in applying its operation to Gertrude or even to Laertes? A superficial observer might seek such logic in the fall of Lear, who cast out Cordelia and Kent, and was in turn cast out by those pelican daughters whose flattery led him to that arbitrary and extreme act. But in the true impact of this great tragedy these things are trifles here; they are merely incidental to more significant matters. Whatever the government of the universe may be, it is certainly not ruled by decorum. The drama, it is true, must seek to make its limited stage-world intelligible. But great drama has windows opening out upon the universe, and reflects its mysteries.

It is reasonably certain that this kind of appropriate justice was not part of Aristotle's theory of *hamartia*, though it is evident enough that this theory involved some satisfaction of a sense of justice as integral to tragedy. When Aristotle's *Poetics* became known to the Western European world, to the Renaissance humanistic world which succeeded to the mediaeval Christian world, the theory was simplified and hardened. It could not well have been otherwise, in a world dominated by God's providence in constant operation. For Roger Ascham, tragedies were 'the goodliest argument of all . . . for the use of a learned preacher.'[1] Aristotle's 'pity and terror' lent themselves to this simple logic which made of tragedy a species of moral *exemplum*. There was pity for undeserved suffering, and terror lest we fall under the condemnation which lights upon the tyrant or the evildoer. It all fitted snugly into a recognised pattern.

We have long been familiar with A. C. Bradley's more complex version of the theory of *hamartia*, which made of it a key, if not to unlock Shakespeare's heart, at least to disclose the hidden sources of reconciliation to tragic conclusions in the heart of the reader of

[1]. *The Schoolmaster*. Ed. Arber. 1876. p. 130.

Shakespeare's tragedies. As Bradley applied the theory, it gained persuasiveness from its presentation in his classical book upon *Shakespearean Tragedy*, from the mind and the imagination of a subtle and philosophic critic who from every quarter illuminated the dramatic poems upon which he was engaged. He was careful not to press too closely his survey of the tragedies in the direction of syllogisms with a constant major premise. Yet that premise remains dominant in the concept of the tragedy of character with an operative 'tragic flaw' or 'fatal flaw,' to use the terms in general usage, though they are a perversion of the Greek word and concept of *hamartia*. For my part, I have never been able to find comfort in this concept, even if I had been able to assent to it.

For the philosopher Hegel, by whom Bradley was deeply influenced, there might be satisfaction in the spectacle of a dispassionately ethical universe avenging deviations from its norms upon the offenders. But if such a spectacle may well evoke terror, and even ill-regulated pity, that very pity is here opposed to the *katharsis*, call it purgation or reconciliation as we will, which was for Aristotle the atmosphere of tragic pleasure. Aristotle's argument indeed, a piece of special pleading, countered Plato's attack upon poetry on ethical grounds with an appeal to a higher court of aesthetic principles, as Bradley well knew.

But even if we could accept a directly ethical basis for tragedy, we should be hard put to it when we apply the principle of the 'tragic flaw' to Shakespeare's tragedies. This indeed is coming into increasingly general agreement of late. Bradley's work has met with severe criticism, if often for the wrong reasons. We find his ethical approach reinforced, for example, and his timidity upbraided, in a full return to Ascham's view. But this is exceptional in the general flow of thought. The 'tragic flaw' has been re-stated, with more respect for the Greek language and for Aristotle, in terms of errors of passion and not of temperament or character. Aristotle's *Poetics* themselves, along with Bradley, have been subjected to a searching criticism which repels all destructive moral analysis of tragic heroism in Greek and Shakespearian tragedy alike.[1]

We are not likely ever to see a return to the absurd dilemma which led to the picking and choosing among Shakespeare's tragedies as witnesses for a preconceived case. The theory of the 'tragic flaw' clearly runs into heavy weather in *Romeo and Juliet,* to take an extreme example. Impatience is a faint and infinitesimal shadow upon the moral horizon, developing beyond all reason into a devastating storm which blackens the sky of Verona and eclipses the sun of youth, the daylight of beauty, and the warmth of true love. The breeding-ground of the storm lies elsewhere than in the nature of the lovers, as the Prologue makes manifest and explicit. A way out of the difficulty was sought by addicts of the theory in the simple exclusion of the play from the category of true tragedy. Thus the tragedy itself, having a fatal flaw, is executed by 'poetic justice' in Pope's sense of the phrase.

But we are not in a much happier case elsewhere in Shakespeare's tragedies. The moral physicians are far from unanimity in their diagnoses of the tragic flaws of their patients. And to all there is an answer, to Hamlet's melancholy or indecision, to Othello's jealous

1. P. Alexander. *Hamlet Father and Son.* 1957.

nature, to the pride of Coriolanus, the anger of Lear, and even to Antony's infatuation or Macbeth's ambition. The heart of Aristotle's doctrine of *katharsis,* in truth, does not lie in this manner of *hamartia,* whether in *Hamlet* or in much of his own material in Greek tragedy, in Sophocles' *Philoctetes* or *Antigone,* for example, both plays barely touched upon by Aristotle. Poetic justice in its usual sense will not serve to purge our emotions, nor to reconcile us to catastrophe. Yet some satisfaction of our sense of justice is necessary if the tragic emotions are not to be heightened and to remain unresolved in a final disharmony.

The theme of justice runs like a coloured thread through the warp and woof of the four major tragedies most plainly for our examination, though all Shakespeare's tragedies alike respond to such an enquiry. If the enquiry is to serve its true purpose, we may not limit ourselves to modern developments of that most complex of ethical concepts, by the exclusion of what was manifestly present and valid in their author's mind and in the minds of their first spectators. We may, for example, find it easy to accept the Elizabethan concept of justice as the expression of order in the cosmos, and yet be disconcerted to find among the implications of this position John Marbecke's definition of justice as varying according to the degree, condition, estate, and person of the individual.[1] Yet this aspect of cosmic order is familiar enough in Shakespeare, and plays its part in *Macbeth* as elsewhere.

---

1. *A Booke of Notes and Commonplaces.* 1581. pp. 569-70.

Public justice:
MACBETH

In its main lines *Macbeth* seems to offer little difficulty, at first sight at any rate. Malcolm summarizes the case for us at the end of the play. Justice has been done upon 'this dead butcher and his fiend-like queen.' Malcolm was not, of course, an unprejudiced observer. But however partial and incomplete his estimate of the great protagonists of this tragedy, we assent without protest to their downfall. Yet there is a marked difference between Shakespeare's history of *Richard the Third* and his tragedy of *Macbeth*, the difference of pity which suffuses terror. It might seem that Hobbes's facile reduction of pity to transferred self-pity is out of place here at least. The German poet and dramatist Grillparzer sought the solution of the problem in the conception of Macbeth and Lady Macbeth as man and woman in the abstract, types of the universal masculine and the universal feminine in their character and their actions. There is thus a natural sympathy for them in all of us who belong to one or the other sex. This suggestion is really only an over-stressing of one part of the truth concerning these two complete and rounded dramatic portraits of a man and a woman. We are moving steadily away, in spite of stage and film, from the concept of *Hamlet* as the tragedy of a man who cannot make up his mind. We may be tempted by a description of *Macbeth* as the tragedy of a man who has his mind made up for him. But we could not accept this notion in the form 'the tragedy of *man* who always has to have his mind made up for him by a woman.' This would obviously not do as an interpretation of *Macbeth*. Yet there is some truth in this approach, and it has its bearings upon the question of tragic pity or tragic sympathy.

There is a very fine distinction to be made in the initial presentation of Macbeth, in his first response to the prophecies of the witches. The question is whether or no they are playing upon a mind that has already considered and half-formulated desperate and ambitious designs. The tendency of late, in criticism as upon the stage, has been to accept this preparation of Macbeth's mind and nature for temptation. Such an interpretation is in harmony with the conception of tragedy as the outcome of a tragic flaw in character, the flaw here being ambition. It also harmonizes with the general modern inexperience of witchcraft, and leads, with a little experience of its able successor, modern psychology in its more spectacular aspects, to the sophisticated notion that the Witches, along with the

Ghost of Banquo, as well as the Dagger, are mere projections of Macbeth's mind, even though Banquo too sees the Witches. It is a common error that to ensure for Shakespeare some significance for reader and stage to-day we must in some measure translate him, in effect, into a modern idiom and atmosphere of thought and experience. Witchcraft, along with the power of evil itself, has sunk to-day to the category of superstitions, of exhibits preserved by history and the Churches of all religions in a kind of museum of an incredible past, to the eyes of all who are narrowly bound within the circle of this limited contemporary world, and who cannot escape from their bonds even by the imagination that suspends disbelief in yielding to dramatic creation. It is a salutary thought that the certain truths of a recent yesterday are the exploded theories of to-day, as with the constitution of matter, and that our cherished certainties of to-day may be the rejected superstitions of to-morrow, in all fields of human thought. The vast majority of readers and spectators of a play of Shakespeare are wisely content to merge themselves in the entrancing exhibition of the universals of human nature, in a setting which their imagination enables them to accept unfettered. The prime fault of a producer of a play of Shakespeare is the refusal to trust his dramatist.

It is well to recall once more that this play moves in the Jacobean age, under a Scottish King who had executed witches for such evil powers and acts as the witches in *Macbeth* boast of on their first appearance. And the scene of the play is set in Scotland, in wild remote country where, as notoriously then in Lancashire, as to-day in Cornwall or even in Warwickshire, such evil phenomena could be observed by believing eyes in full operation. The *Book of Common Prayer* then as now provided in the Litany a prayer for daily use for delivery from 'the crafts and assaults of the devil,' of which witchcraft was one potent instrument. There is no sign of Macbeth's dangerous ambition until after his first interview with the witches. And even then Lady Macbeth diagnoses him coolly as 'not without ambition.'[1]

Much play has been made with the argument that the Weird Sisters do not in fact tempt Macbeth to evil designs upon Duncan, but only prophesy a future in which he rises to the kingship. To the Elizabethan, this is mere hair-splitting, and the law was decisive on the question. To 'imagine' the death of the sovereign, to prophesy evil to the sovereign, was a capital offence, indistinguishable from conspiracy to bring about such disastrous events. The temptation was implicit in the prophecy, as any Elizabethan would understand.

We must moreover consider from an Elizabethan standpoint the nature of the crime in which Macbeth becomes involved, and before which he naturally hesitates. As in *Hamlet,* so here it is not merely murder, it is regicide. But here the King is no usurper. It would be dangerous to conceive, or to present on the stage of James's London, and before James himself and his Court, the story of a nobleman who moved by human passions only, by human motives, could plot and execute this ultimate crime. James, like Duncan, was legitimate King of Scotland. He had seen his father murdered, and the Gowrie Conspiracy aimed at him-

---

1. Bradley no less coolly dismisses her many significant comments upon his character: 'his wife . . . did not fully understand him' (p. 351), in the interests of his own interpretation.

self as he believed. Gunpowder Plot and its aftermath at that very time were busying the Court of Star Chamber. It was necessary to attribute such a design to more than human engineering. Even where an ordinary felony was concerned, the formal indictment of the accused was couched in the words

> *deum pre oculis suis non habens sed instigacione diabolica motus et seductus.*

The phrase 'moved and *seduced*' by devilish instigation is significant. The crime of Macbeth, like that of Guy Fawkes, was not merely diabolical, not merely the yieldings of Macbeth to temptation. It was the outcome of a diabolical conspiracy, a deliberate assault initiated by the Devil working through his instruments, the Witches. And from this craft and this assault Macbeth is not delivered.

The very first scene of the play presents the Witches, with thunder and lightning, signs of the hellish world of chaos and destruction that lies beneath the perilously balanced order of the universe of man. They are to meet Macbeth presently, a first meeting that *they* are seeking, under orders. It is decisive for the interpretation of the action and significance of the play, as of Macbeth's character. It has been suggested that this first scene requires a previous scene, with Macbeth already preparing for his crime, and that this, with other apparent gaps in the play, illustrates the incompleteness of the surviving text. This to my mind is merely a re-writing of Shakespeare and his play, on the assumption that Macbeth is by nature criminally ambitious and villainous. The only conceivable further introduction to the play as we have it would indeed be a Prologue in Hell. One could almost wish that Shakespeare had done it.

It is this, indeed, that makes it possible for Macbeth to be a truly tragic figure, in the sense that pity and terror are alike aroused and are consistent with submission to the catastrophe. But for this, we should be at a loss to understand Shakespeare's insistence upon the great excellencies of Macbeth in the opening scenes, in which he comes close to the perfection of Hamlet in Ophelia's eyes. A loyal subject, a man of nobility in all things, a great soldier who is yet free from ruthlessness, the picture is almost overdrawn, and certainly has no tinge of irony. It is, with equal certainty, intentional that in this picture King Duncan, the Lords of Scotland, and the soldiers and common people are of one mind about Macbeth. Macbeth was a great prize, worth winning for his own sake as for the issues at stake in the winning. And he proved to be hard to win. 'The more we increase in faith and virtuous living,' wrote Sir John Cheke, 'the more strongly will Satan assault us.' This is the deep significance of the words that Shakespeare puts into Macbeth's mouth immediately after the murder of Duncan:

> Had I but died an hour before this chance,
> I had lived a blessed time.

We may not take these words, with what follows, as hypocritical, designed merely to meet the situation and to mislead. They do so, of course. But they spring directly out of Macbeth's true nature, which he has outraged in his desperate deed.

Yet there is that in Macbeth's nature that promises success in the assault upon him. The deeply poetic and imaginative cast of his mind, no rare thing in great captains, makes him receptive to all that is metaphysical, not of this world of reality, to hallucination as to the Weird Sisters. This it is and not the preparation of his own previous thoughts, that makes him amenable to their influence, where Banquo the practical man holds aloof in sceptical questioning. William Perkins in his *Cases of Conscience*[1] specifically names imagination as a contributory factor to the seductions of evil. It might well seem then that Macbeth's virtues and the exceptional qualities of his mind set him in the rank of true heroes of tragedy, and are the source of the tragic pity that is a component part of our acceptance of his fate, without any questioning of the verdict of justice. So, over and over again, an Elizabethan felon on the very scaffold declares, even as he confesses to devilish instigation, penitent, burdened by his conscience, that he is satisfied with the operation of the law. The responsibility is his, and justice must be done lest that chaos return which is the absence of all justice. There remains for such a felon the hope and trust in God's final mercy.

I said that Macbeth was hard to win. From Holinshed onwards the influence of Lady Macbeth was crucial. 'His wife lay sore upon him to attempt the thing.' And Donwald, whose story contributed to Shakespeare's version of the *Macbeth* story, 'abhorred the act greatly in heart, yet through instigation of his wife' agreed to murder King Duff. In the five stages of

---

1. I. vii. 1. (1608)

submission to temptation which the divines recognise,[1] reception, enticement, consent, commission, and habit, the fatal dividing line comes with consent, with the formation of purpose. Up to this point, even a Saint Paul might yield, but no further. And it is at this point that Macbeth's resistance is overcome, and overcome by Lady Macbeth.

Not that this could be pleaded in mitigation for Macbeth in any Elizabethan court. On the contrary, critically-minded Elizabethans with a bowing acquaintance with Aristotle would probably diagnose one of Macbeth's tragic flaws as being unnatural submissiveness to a woman's will. When Adam put up this plea in Milton's *Paradise Lost* to God the Son, he met with a pretty smart rebuke. And Spenser deals at considerable length and with great severity with the submission of Sir Artegall himself, the Knight of Justice, to the Amazon Radigund. The condemnation is none the less because Adam was moved by love and Artegall by love of beauty and by magnanimity. The relations between Macbeth and Lady Macbeth are indeed the key to this play, and they strongly affect the operation of tragic justice on a level far above the simpler logic of *hamartia*. It helps if we shift the emphasis of our thought from the tragedy of Macbeth to the tragedy of Lady Macbeth, and in so doing move as far away from the concept of a 'fiend-like queen' as we have moved from that of a 'dead butcher.'

Is there anywhere in literature a more rounded or a more affecting picture of the intimacy and mutual confidence of husband and wife? There is an amazing touch in the Sleep-walking scene, when Lady Macbeth

---

1. W. Perkins. 'A Treatise of Predestination.' *Works* (1613) II, pp. 635-6.

mutters to herself and to the absent, remote Macbeth who haunts her waking dreams:

> Wash your hands, put on your night-gown; look not so pale. I tell you yet again, Banquo's buried; he cannot come out on's grave.

'I tell you *yet again.*' How often have these two talked together once they were alone; how often has she had to reassure him, strengthen him, give her courage to him. We seem to know far more than the play has time to show us explicitly in action and dialogue. Or see how Shakespeare shows us Lady Macbeth working upon Macbeth before his dread decision to murder Duncan. As Professor Kittredge once put it vividly, she uses three arguments, the three stock arguments of a woman with a man, especially of a wife with a husband. 'You would do it if you dared—but you daren't.' 'You would do it if you loved me—but you don't.' And finally, 'If I were a man, I'd do it myself.' 'I am settled,' says Macbeth—and no wonder! The essential normality of the Macbeth we are so clearly shown fits him for a close and intimate partnership with a woman. He attaches a high value to the social amenities, to love, to honour, to 'troops of friends,' to 'golden opinions from all sorts of people.' We might fancy that we see something of Shakespeare himself in this, as in his merciful humanity as a soldier, and in his sensitive, over-active imagination. To such a man his inevitable Eve, who is essentially feminine even in her rejection of her femininity, remote indeed from that Goneril who bullied the Duke of Albany. Lady Macbeth's being was bound up with Macbeth's at all points. Her ambition is all for him, and she stands by his side, doing violence to her own nature until it breaks under the strain. And here, in this great play, we diverge from all formal, official, theological analyses of human action.

The most tragic aspect of the whole play may well seem to be that in which we may look upon it as the loss of their paradise by these two, a more poignant tragedy than Milton's. For in the end of the poem Adam and Eve unparadised pass through the gates hand in hand, taking their solitary way together. Dante too, relegating Paolo and Francesca to the Inferno befitting their sin, leaves them still in company. Francesca is still and for ever with him 'who never from me shall be parted,' as the winds of hell blow them to and fro. But Shakespeare was more ruthless. The crime of Macbeth and Lady Macbeth brings separation between them, gradually, fatally, finally. And this separation develops, widens, and is made complete in measure as retribution approaches and at last overwhelms them. They meet their fates severally, and in a terrible solitude and darkness of the spirit with an unpassable gulf fixed between them.[1]

This separation is amazingly portrayed in the play. It arises in a measure out of the character of Macbeth; it runs parallel to the development of this character; and it is one of the fundamental causes of the shattering of Lady Macbeth's mind and spirit. Once the initial, decisive crime is committed, and Macbeth has gone over to the powers of evil, he begins to withdraw himself into the fastnesses of his own darkening mind, into a solitary world of his own thoughts, imagination, and

---

1. It is a rare instance of insensitiveness in Bradley that he observes merely that 'they drift a little apart.' (p. 350).

will. 'All causes shall give way.' Surely the beginning of this separation is marked already in Act II. Sc. 2, as soon as the murder is committed. Lady Macbeth, meeting him, cries out, '*My husband!*' But he answers grimly, 'I have done the deed.' She is wrapped up in him from beginning to end. But he is already deep in the deed. For her the murder, and their ambitions, are part and parcel of their common life. But Macbeth does not think of it in terms of husband and wife. He keeps his own counsel for the manner and time of the slaying of Banquo and Fleance, lost in his own imaginings, in Act III. Sc. 2. She is already at arm's length from him. The decision is his alone, and he is no longer under her guidance and tutelage. She still shares his burden with him and is his partner, as far as Act III. Sc. 4, in the Banquet scene, when the appalling effect on Macbeth of the apparition of Banquo's ghost threatens to make him betray himself, and she strives to save the situation. 'Are you a man?' is her cry again. She was still his 'sweet remembrancer' just before this, but these are the last words of love she was to hear from him. From now on she is an intruder upon his dark and secret thoughts, as the end of this scene plainly shows. What is apparently dialogue is mainly soliloquy interrupted by abrupt questions.

And from that night on, as far as the play shows, they never meet again; the separation is complete. In Act IV. Sc. 1 Macbeth is alone; he is taking counsel with the Witches now, and his counsel is not shared with Lady Macbeth, who, be it observed, never comes into contact with the Witches. She is, indeed, a subsidiary force in the seducing of Macbeth. In Act V. Sc. 1 she is alone, walking in her sleep, speaking strange matters, her thoughts and her words beyond her control. It is an amazing scene of virtuosity in the portrayal of a nervous breakdown, as we should now call it. Lady Macbeth is capable of terrific self-control in emergency, stronger than Macbeth. Her faint in Act II. Sc. 3, a genuine faint, occurs when the crisis has come, has been met, and is over. Macbeth is now doing very well. She is not needed further, and she gives way to the strain. A very woman in all ways, she is never more so than in her physical revulsion from blood. In this scene, her fainting follows hot upon Macbeth's vivid evocation of images of blood. In her sleep-walking her ruined mind is haunted by the gush of the old man Duncan's blood, and nauseated by the smell of blood upon her uncleansable hands.

Macbeth has no need of her now. She will never be needed again. And she is entirely dependent upon him and identified with him. The purpose and springs of her life are broken. The temporary physical weakness of the earlier scene is transformed into the permanent breakdown of her mind and spirit. In her sleep-walking her thoughts are still on him, and she lives over once again the scenes in which their life came to this pass, addressing herself throughout and solely to him. We hear how in her sleep she writes letters, to whom if not to Macbeth, 'since his majesty went into the field'? She must seek to share her thoughts, her fears; she must express them or perish. Her separation in soul from Macbeth has closed her only normal outlet. Macbeth was out and about, busy with his wars, in his true element, a soldier at his trade. But she was cooped up, powerless, unoccupied. If it is not good for man to be alone, it is infinitely worse for a woman, repugnant to the more social structure of her nature, the purpose and conditions of her existence. How much more if to this is added an outcast solitariness of spirit, with no warm heart to nestle into.

So it is that this exclusion in spirit from Macbeth is a profound cause of her sleep-walking, of her 'slumbery agitation.' Her 'infected mind' had only her deaf pillows to discharge her secrets to, and the weak solace of tears, it would seem, was not for her. It is surely more than a coincidence that the last words of her sleep-walking are a reminiscence of the last words that we hear Macbeth say to her, 'Come, we'll to sleep.' Lady Macbeth leaves us muttering, 'To bed, to bed, to bed,' a last poor memory of the vanished hours when she and Macbeth were safe and were together, husband and wife, in the comfortable dark, before she craved for lights continually in her solitude.

For Macbeth she is now her Doctor's patient; her 'thick-coming fancies' were for him to 'cure her of that.' And at the very end this tragedy of Lady Macbeth is consummated with a great crying-out of women within; she is dying, still alone, with her unblessed tapers burning. When Macbeth hears the news he has already 'supped full with horrors.'

> *Seaton*   The Queen, my lord, is dead.
> *Macbeth* She should have died hereafter,
> There would have been a time for such a word.

'She would have died some day, sooner or later, when I might have known and felt what is was to lose a wife. But death is upon us all. Mortality makes a mock of all human affairs, and love *is* Time's fool. I am tied to a stake, and so are all men, and all women.' So in a mood of black despair he goes on to that dreadful comment upon life and human love which is made so much more deeply tragic when we recall the moment and the cause of its utterance. In the very rhythm of this speech, if truly heard or justly spoken, we hear the slow measured beat of a passing-bell for Lady Macbeth, and we are appalled by so disastrous an epitaph upon her passing. It is also a passing-bell for Macbeth, and an epitaph upon himself.

The operation of justice, both human and divine, is manifest in the course of the catastrophe of this play, and it is unquestioned, without mitigation of sentence or plea for mercy. We may not distinguish between the two protagonists and seek to plead for Macbeth because of his courage or for any other reason. Both are involved in an equal condemnation, from which there is no appeal. On behalf of human justice, Malcolm passes judgment, the voice as also the instrument of that public justice which has been delegated to him as rightful King of Scotland and which lawfully triumphs over Macbeth in his hands. No other conclusion could be tolerable, unless the estate of the world were to be undone, to use Macbeth's own phrase. His crimes are deadly, regicide, murder, usurpation, and tyranny. Lady Macbeth is accessory before and after his crimes, and shares with him in their fruits, full partner at all points. She never comes to that justice, taking her own life and anticipating her certain fate.

There is no room for pity here, it would seem. And none for mercy in the application of divine justice either, despite the potent instigation of the powers of evil. The Elizabethans were accustomed to a theological approach to the problems of life, and were well informed in the main truths of their Christian faith. They were aware, and Shakespeare was aware, that while the Devil had permission to tempt man, yet no man might be tempted beyond his powers of resistance. The choice to yield or to resist remained his own responsibility, and by his free choice he was judged.[1] Macbeth's yielding, upon the further pressure of Lady Macbeth, was a sin as well as an error, inasmuch as submission to a woman's will went contrary to the divinely established order of the universe. As for Lady Macbeth, theologically at least the weaker vessel and by her nature more subject to dangerous thoughts, herself inviting and invoking evil spirits, her obstinacy not only helped to damn Macbeth but fought against her natural adviser and stay, her husband.

So we see in both classical examples of the development of evil in human life, in all its recognised stages. After consent and commission comes use and habit, and finally the culminating stage of despair, the deepest of sins. And all these stages are plainly portrayed in action and dialogue in the play. It has been suggested by Professor Hardin Craig[2] that in Lady Macbeth's sleep-walking we see the operation of God's

---

[1]. It is this, if nothing else, that makes impossible Bradley's interpretation of Banquo as also ensnared by the Weird Sisters. 'The Witches and his own ambition have conquered him.' But his attitude is consistent throughout with firm resistance. Whatever truth may appear to lie in their prophecies, he will for himself keep 'My bosom franchised and allegiance clear.' He stands 'in the great hand of God.' Early in the play, late at night, when he is heavy with sleep, a time for evil thoughts assaulting the best of men, he calls upon divine power for help. The need he feels is ominous of the stream of evil directed at another, at Macbeth, that night and in that place. The business of the Weird Sisters is with Macbeth, as they plainly say. Macbeth's attitude is strongly contrasted with Banquo's. He can contemplate jumping the life to come, even before he consents to his fatal crime. It is, moreover, relevant that Banquo was the ancestor of King James, who saw the play.

[2]. *The Enchanted Glass* (1936) p. 120.

judgment falling upon her, a visitation of God. But it is abundantly explained in the natural order of her life. Both know well enough where they stand. 'Hell is murky,' says Lady Macbeth. And Macbeth has given his eternal jewel to the common enemy of man. He has lost his soul and his hope of salvation. Neither is even capable of repentance at the eleventh hour. The twelfth hour awaits them irrevocably. This is not felony, it is damnation.

Are Macbeth and Lady Macbeth then portrayed in this play as moral *exempla*? Does the heart of the tragedy lie in the pity and terror evoked by the fall of a dead butcher and a fiend-like queen? Are we purged of these emotions solely by the spectacle of public justice in satisfactory operation, and by the prospect of the divine judgment to come? It is most manifestly not so. There is no place for pity in such a spectacle. And there is no recognisable form of *katharsis* in the mere ravening of the hunters after wild beasts at bay. Pity and terror alike reside here in the corruption of a man and a woman of whom we had every reason to look for great and good things. Their downfall is due no less to their qualities than to their defects, to all that makes each complete and full man and woman, to Macbeth's high spirit, to the power and complexity of his intellect and imagination, to the depth of Lady Macbeth's single-minded merging of her desires in the advancement of her husband, and to the absorption of their love one for another. That such fair and good traits of nature should come to such a pass is matter indeed for pity and terror in the general mind surveying their history. It might appear that the universe has gone awry, that the stars are not fixed in their spheres. But in the end, as pity and terror increase, the certainty grows with them that the ancient pillars of justice, upon which the universe rests, are immovable. 'O that a man might plead for a man with God, as a man pleadeth for a neighbour,' cried Job. We are content even in our perturbation not to plead for Macbeth and Lady Macbeth, either at the bar of public justice or at the mercy-seat of divine judgment.

But they *were* our neighbours, it seems, before they became estranged from us as from each other. Are they not our neighbours still at the end, as Iago is not, and Richard the Third and Goneril are not? We think we know the absolute Macbeth, and there is something of the changeling in the Macbeth presented to the world in desperate career. He is transformed despite himself by the power of evil, though that power, as always, draws into its stream of influence his own strength, his great spirit, his honour, his imagination. But he is still in all essentials the Macbeth we first met. Even when tied to a stake, at the very end, he would fain be merciful to Macduff, being certain of overcoming him, rather than add to his guilt of blood.

A star may be observed increasing in magnitude and light into a portent of brightness in the night sky, then vanishing, destroyed by its own explosion. But the sky is the poorer for its disappearance from among the strong unchanging stars which never shot madly from their spheres. To the understanding eye there is no spectacle of greater awe, and to the understanding heart none of more moving pitifulness.

Private justice:
OTHELLO

The tragedy of *Othello* has occasioned a good deal of unrest among those who have made it their business to write commentaries upon Shakespeare's plays. This unrest may take the mild form of expressing distaste or pain, or the more explosive comments of neo-classical criticism. Catastrophic events in private and domestic life, as distinguished from events which have their source in the wider world of national life, are felt to be less proper to tragedy as to epic, and a play resting upon so limited a theme may border perilously upon melodrama, lacking universal significance. *Othello*, wrote A. C. Bradley, is 'less symbolic' than *Macbeth*, *King Lear*, or *Hamlet*.

Some trends in recent criticism of the play have swiftly redressed the balance by symbolical interpretations in the modern fashion which seem to make of it a companion-piece to *Macbeth* with its powers of evil in the form of the Weird Sisters. For one critic, Othello is the human soul struggling towards the Good, the Better Self. Iago is the corroding influence within Othello's nature which corrupts him, the Worse Self. The dramatic conflict lies between the Better Self and the Worse. The play is thus a moral allegory. For another, Othello is Man in the abstract, Iago is the Devil, and Desdemona is Divinity. Iago is thus pure and absolute malignity or evil, the spirit of denial. So the play is a theological allegory. One may well boggle at Divinity in the shape of Desdemona telling fibs. But it is more repugnant to the very soul of tragedy to translate its action and characters into bodiless abstractions.

It is evident, for example, that to envisage *Othello* as a play moving entirely in a moral world, or a spiritual world, excludes all thought of justice other than divine justice, whose operation is beyond our pity, if not our terror, and in which it would be presumptuous alike to seek, or to fail to find, the purgation of our emotions. It is abundantly clear, on the contrary, that in *Othello* we see the principle of private justice in disastrous usurpation. It is well to note that in Shakespeare's source for the play, in Cinthio's novel, there is some hint of such a theme. In it, there is criminal conspiracy between Othello and Iago, and Iago is Desdemona's actual murderer. The punishment of their crimes is in the hands of public justice, and is inadequate. Private justice therefore takes over in the vengeful killing of Othello by Desdemona's family. Iago goes scot-free as far as this crime is concerned, though Emilia, who survives to tell the story, reports his later downfall. The story indeed presented Shakespeare with a tangle of loose ends to be wound afresh before they could be bound into unity. But, crude as it was in all ways, it sufficed to set his imagination to work. Was this theme of justice part of its impact upon him?

There is perhaps some profit in seeking to retrace the possible process of the operation of that imagination. Of the four major tragedies *Othello* gives us the best opportunity for so doing. The skeleton-stories of the others offered less freedom. They were known and familiar from chronicle or earlier play, and they bore encrustations and accretions from the past which could not altogether be ignored. He went as far as he dared with *King Lear,* as with *Measure for Measure* in comedy. But with *Othello* he had a free hand. The story was pure fiction, and was not familiar from repetition. How then did Shakespeare set to work?

I once put a question to a very distinguished composer, Sir Alexander Mackenzie, after lunch at the Royal Academy of Music, of which he was then Principal, and I Professor of Poetics. 'How does it begin?' I asked, 'what is the starting-point of one of your quartets, for example?' Sir Alexander was a Scotsman, and chary of words. He pondered, then slowly replied, 'Ach well, ye see, ye get an *idea,*' and he evidently considered the discussion closed, the question settled. But after a while, and after further pondering, more enlightenment came. 'Then, of course, ye work the idea out. And it works itself out.' And now, with the thunder of Scottish consonants, the oracle fell silent for good.

A rival account of the conception of a work of art is given in a novel of Quiller-Couch, critic as well as creative writer:

> You can't call it idling when you sit—say in the Bois, on any chance bench anywhere—seeing nothing, letting the carriages go by like an idle show of phenomena, but with your whole soul thrilling to a new idea, drinking it in, pushing out new fibres which grow as they suck in more of it through small new ducts, with a ripple and again a choke and yet again a gurgle, which you orchestrate into a sound of deep waters combining as you draw them home— Oh yes, you may laugh, but I know what conception is: what Shakespeare felt like when he sat one night in a garden, and the great plot of *Othello* came teeming.[1]

Here again is the *idea,* working itself out in the whole soul, until the great plot 'comes teeming.' It is very much what Matthew Arnold said: 'The poet has in the first place to select an excellent action.' Without such an 'action,' no skill in treatment can overcome this incurable defect. We are perhaps much too apt today, even in considering Aristotle, to think of an *idea* and of an *action* as being disparate terms in drama, since the modern drama so often begins with an abstract problem and continues with the invention of a group of characters and a series of events, the idea clothed in an action in those senses of the words. But with the greatest drama, Greek or Shakespearean, no such distinction is possible, or if made can only be artificial and tendentious, within the sum-total of thought, character, and events, which are members one of another in one body. We may well wonder how

---

1. *Foe-Farrell,* pp. 110-11 (Collins)

an 'excellent action,' in Arnold's phrase, could have arisen from the reading of Cinthio's novel, even by Shakespeare.

How did Shakespeare begin, having read the story in Cinthio? We may imagine him proceeding in a mechanical way, working out on the basis of the story a scenario, a sort of scaffolding for a new building upon this design translated into the terms of the stage. If so, he would in due course have arrived at Act Five. In Cinthio, it is night. Othello and Desdemona are in bed together. Iago is hidden in a closet in their bedroom, and presently makes a noise, as arranged. Othello bids Desdemona get up and see what is wrong. Iago rushes out and strikes her down with a sandbag. To hide their crime they pull down the ceiling upon her body: it passes as an accident. But Othello, overcome by remorse, breaks with Iago and dismisses him, and Iago now accuses Othello publicly of the murder of Cassio and of Desdemona. This would indeed have yielded only material for Rymer's famous denunciation of Shakespeare's *Othello* as 'a bloody farce without salt or savour.' It could not have been thus that Shakespeare proceeded. It can hardly be doubted that such a scenario or 'plot' in the Elizabethan sense was the first stage in the actual composition of the play. But it is certain that an intense activity of incubation preceded Shakespeare's first putting of pen to paper, something like the process that Quiller-Couch describes. Perhaps the metaphors of conception and gestation are more proper to such a process of imaginative creation.

Few will doubt, I believe, that Shakespeare's primary interest lay in men and women, rather than in abstract concepts. He had, after all, been an actor before he became a dramatist, and continued acting well into the middle at least of his great career. It is the business of an actor, on being allotted a part to play, to create a man or a woman out of the dialogue and action as he finds it in his script, to project on the screen of his imagination a body, a voice, and a spirit, which he will present on the stage in due course. For Shakespeare, Cinthio's novel was a kind of script, from which he sought to project men and women of significance and truth to human nature. He was not, fortunately, bound by his script. But from that script, a prosaic, matter-of-fact, newspaper story about people who were nameless except for Desdemona, he drew something that he had already found in the stories of Julius Caesar and of Hamlet, a conflict of human souls, of soul against soul, of soul against circumstance, of soul against itself, but this time of souls moved to their utmost depths by the most shattering of human passions that affect men in their private lives, by pride, jealousy, and revengefulness. So in his silent, solitary meditations, the printed book pushed away from him, the shadow of certain men and women gradually took shape upon the screen of his thoughts, the essential work of dramatic creation.

So the idea was born in Shakespeare's busy, dreaming mind, some concept of the two great opponents, Othello like a stately, dark-sailed, ocean-going galleon, beflagged, thrusting under her fore-foot great surges; Iago like a sinister, quick-sailing, crafty, dangerous pirate-galley. And with this, the dreadful vision of the reefs upon which such a noble galleon might be driven to final shipwreck. Something like this happened to

Shakespeare, as he let this queer Italian story set him thinking and feeling. This was Arnold's 'action,' in which was involved also the grievous fate of Desdemona. It is all in Othello's phrase, 'it is the cause, it is the cause,' and Shakespeare saw it looming up like a great black cloud with thunder and lightning in its wake, matter for tragic treatment. But with Shakespeare imagination and intellect worked in indissoluble partnership, and the conflict of thought was inseparable from a conflict of persons. There has been great debate upon the focus of intellectual principle in Shakespeare's treatment of this story.

I have mentioned, only to dismiss them, two allegorical interpretations of this intellectual background. A third, slavishly tracing the operation of *hamartia,* of the 'tragic flaw,' survives still despite Bradley's uncompromising rejection of 'the ridiculous notion that Othello was jealous by temperament,' along with its elaboration as a study of Moorish blood and Oriental social traditions. A fourth interpretation, harping upon the Moorishness of Othello, offers the play as inspired by the problem of the Moor, the coloured man, at odds with an alien society and race, something of a parallel to Shakespeare's treatment of Shylock in *The Merchant of Venice,* similarly interpreted.

We may think it probable that Shakespeare, as his play progressed, had talks about it with some of his fellows in his company, with Richard Burbage and John Lowin for example. Of course he had Burbage, the first Hamlet in the long history of that great part, in his mind's eye for his new tragic hero, and Lowin, who had played Claudius, for his new villain. Can we think it likely that he would put it to Burbage in this fashion, revealing this conception of the core of his play?—

> 'I have a new play in the making, a tragedy, and there will be a notable part for you in it, the part of a jealous man. What do you say?'

But a jealous man is faintly ludicrous. The company had already had the comic Ford in *The Merry Wives*. We may well hear Burbage humming and hawing, the words 'my public expects' trembling on his lips. Or was it in this fashion?—

> 'What say you to the part of a noble soldier, a general in the Venetian wars, beloved by a beautiful daughter of Venice. He is practised upon by a cunning Italian, a dangerous Italian' (with a side-glance at Lowin), 'to think her unchaste, and slays her in his passion. Yet she is innocent, and oh the pity of it! For he is a man without guile, where the Italian is all guile. It happened at Cyprus, before the Turks took it. Did I say he was a Moor?'
> ' A Moor do you say?'
> 'Yes, it is so in the book, and truly he must be a Moor. A princely Moor, a king among men, and therefore the more a child against Italian subtleties.'

What tragic actor would fail to be stirred by such a sketch of a new part? And I think I see a sinister smile gleaming for a moment in Lowin's practised face. I think also that Burbage's next question would be a very natural one.

> 'Under what name do I play the noble Moorish general?'

And doubtless Lowin was no less curious.

Let this not be thought to be a frivolous or merely pedantic question, for them or for us to-day. There is much matter in a name, and Shakespeare gave more heed to names than we are apt to think. There is room for a very instructive book on the subject. Why, for example, did Shakespeare choose the name of Katherine for Lady Percy, whose historical name was Eleanor, rejecting the authority of Holinshed who gives her name and lineage?[1] The answer may seem clear, after his two previous Katherines in comedy, brave and witty girls both. Dare we think that his choice of Angelo in *Measure for Measure*, replacing the Promos of his source, reveals depths of irony and gives a clue to the idea out of which this play arose? Are any significances to be truly observed in the names of the characters in *Othello*?

The only name which Cinthio's story offered Shakepeare was Desdemona, which he adopted gratefully. Even if he did not know that the name means one fated to misfortune—though I think he would enquire —nevertheless it is a striking name, it is music and music-making. Cassio is a familiar Italian name. We need look for no significance from his previous use of the same name in its Roman form for the 'lean and hungry Cassius,' except perhaps to assure us that Cassio is a patrician. Iago is an odd name to give to an Italian and a Venetian, for it is a common Spanish name, the Spanish form of James. One may indeed wonder what King James thought of this choice, as later on when he saw the Italian form of his name, Iachimo (Giacomo), as the villain in *Cymbeline*. Iago

---

[1]. *Chronicles 1577*. p. 1136. Modern historians say her name was in fact Elizabeth.

II: PRIVATE JUSTICE [36]

obviously has in him a great deal of the Elizabethan Englishman's idea of the Spaniard, jealous, vain, coldly passionate, stoical, intriguing, unscrupulous. Roderigo, it will be observed, a character of contemptible quality, also bears a Spanish name.

It is not irrelevant to recall here Shakespeare's first sketch for the Moor of Venice, the Prince of Morocco, in *The Merchant of Venice,* who also came 'from men of royal siege,' and is there contrasted with the ludicrous Prince of Arragon. And it is well to remember that the Moors, like the English, were hereditary enemies of the Spaniards. The Moorish Kingdom of Granada lasted until 1492. In Shakespeare's adult life the Moors themselves were expelled from Spain, in mass expulsions carried out in 1598 and again in 1609, not long before and not long after the date of *Othello.* The expelled Moors were carried over into Africa, as I have found from Chancery records, mainly in English ships, whose sailors showed great sympathy for the sufferings of these lamentable passengers. And a large and profitable trade was steadily carried on between England and Morocco at this time. It is difficult not to feel, in the conflict between Othello and Iago, some colour of the quarrel that divided the world then, in which the English and the Moors were alike opposed to the common enemy, Spain.

If the name of Iago was something like an instinctive choice, arising out of such undercurrents of thought and feeling, the name of Othello remains baffling. We have long since abandoned the notion of its origin in a Venetian family, the 'Moro dei Otelli,' a recent fiction invented for the purpose. And we now know from Venetian archives that in the story of real life in 1544, re-told by Cinthio in 1565, the Othello was 'Francisco de Sessa dictus Maurus' or 'dictus el Moro.' He was a Venetian, and 'Moro' was only his nickname, from campaigns against the Moors, or from his dark complexion. Iago's real name was Alessandro della Mirandola, who ended by going mad in prison. There is nothing to help us here.

Shakespeare clearly put his hero in a class far above Cinthio's 'Moorish Captain.' He is of royal ancestry, and is a general who speaks for Venice in Cyprus. In Cyprus indeed he *is* Venice, and governs in her name. This Moor has moved far away from Shakespeare's first Moor, Aaron in *Titus Andronicus.* Aaron's friend Mulay bears a Moorish name, even if Aaron does not, and both are Musulmans, misbelievers, like the 'malignant and turbaned Turk' whom Othello slew in Aleppo once. Othello is a Christian hero, sworn enemy to the Turks who were a menace to Venice. Some Moorish names were well-known to Londoners then, on the stage as in real life. But such names as Mulay Mahomet or Abdelmelec or the like could not serve for Othello, nor any modification that might yet hint at Islam. I think it not impossible that Shakespeare hit upon a solution of his difficult problem in the course of his wide reading of Plutarch, with which he was much engaged during these years of dramatic activity. There he would find the name of a Roman emperor, Otho, and near it, on the same page, that of his successor Vitellius. The union of these two, with an Italian conclusion, gave a compounded name of Roman dignity and exotic colour, not too remote from the name of an Italian family known to England, Ottilio. The Emperor Otho was a soldier who, like Othello, when the time came to unarm, his life ruined, turned his own sword upon his undefeated heart. If this, or something like this, was the process of Shakespeare's invention of the name, it was certainly not unapt to his hero, and not irrelevant to his conception of his personality.

Nor is it irrelevant to the question of Othello's race and colour, so much debated. Much has been made, as by A. C. Bradley, of the certainty that Aaron in *Titus Andronicus* is a negro, and is a Moor. Peacham's well-known drawing of a scene in the play bears out all the clear indications of the dialogue. But when we come to Shakespeare's next Moor, the Prince of Morocco, there is equal certainty in the opposite direction. The original stage-direction from Shakespeare's own hand in the authoritative First Quarto of *The Merchant of Venice* runs 'Enter Morochus, a tawny Moor all in white,' and it survives in the First Folio. His retinue is also of this stage pattern, as is clearly stated there. In 1600, as the *Hatfield Papers* record, an Ambassador from Morocco came to visit Queen Elizabeth. The visit does not appear to have been observed by political or diplomatic history. But a portrait of the Moorish envoy, recently discovered in private hands, survives as further evidence. Expert opinion certifies its genuineness as a contemporary painting. And it bears the name of the envoy, and the date. The envoy is of an aristocratic Arab type of countenance, bearded and moustached, with hazel eyes, and wearing a white robe.[1]

It is well to recall also a phrase from *Love's Labour's Lost*, 'many a knight from tawny Spain,' suggesting

---

1. The portrait is now in the possession of the Shakespeare Institute of the University of Birmingham, at Stratford-upon-Avon. See *Shakespeare Survey* 11, pp. 89-97.

that Spaniards and Moors may be dark-complexioned in the same degree. The Elizabethans were familiar with the distinction between 'tawny Moors' and 'black Moors' among the peoples of Africa who were all 'Moors.' The dividing line, also well known, was the river Senegal, from the north of which came the tawny Moors, as the many sailors and traders who dealt with North Africa and West Africa could freely report. Those who traded to West Africa, indeed, were quite precise in their distinction between the two races, between the 'Moor' or 'Arab' on the one hand, and the 'Negro' on the other hand. The word 'Fulvie' is used apparently for those of mixed race, or perhaps for Berbers as distinct from their Arab conquerors. These indications are plain, for example, in the reports of sailors taking part in the voyage which led to the first English discovery of Timbuctoo by Richard Brocket in 1618, who was killed on his return journey to Goa.[1]

The indications that Othello is of the 'black Moor' race and type come from his enemies in the play, from Brabantio, Iago, and Roderigo, and even these are far from decisive. In sum, I can consider nothing so unlikely as that Shakespeare, having imagined his Prince of Morocco, should have reverted to Aaron in his conception of Othello, a great Moorish general of Venice who came 'from men of royal siege.'

It is clear that this has its bearings upon the idea or ideas underlying the play. The production of the play with the great negro actor and singer Paul Robeson emphasized an atmosphere of thought and emotion, a modern atmosphere of social and political problems of

1. P.R.O. C24/491/77. The documents are as yet unpublished.

the present day, in accordance with the fourth interpretation referred to above. A. C. Bradley is more elusive and non-committal than some of his critics allow for, but there can be little doubt where he stands here. For Bradley, Othello must be considered and envisaged as a negro Moor, if only to do full justice to Desdemona's romantic passion. In this, we have 'to rise to Shakespeare's meaning,' in Bradley's own phrase, to see the universal brotherhood of man in an extreme case vindicated by a woman's perceptive love. But the truth is that racial prejudice, as distinct from national enmity or religious enmity, was no problem of Shakespeare's day. In *The Merchant of Venice* it is obvious that the Prince of Morocco is a perfectly proper candidate for Portia's hand, whatever personal preference she may have.[1] Othello's race and colour are accidentals in the main surge of events and thoughts in this play, exploited mainly by Iago for his own ends. Iago, indeed, is the true key to the play and to the conflict between him and Othello which, with its consequences, form the action.

Coleridge's famous diagnosis of Iago's 'motiveless malignity,' revived recently in the form of evil in the abstract in symbolical interpretations of the play and its characters, ignores plain facts. It would not, indeed, take much of a change of emphasis and treatment of story and character to swing some considerable measure of sympathy to Iago's side. He has motive enough, and Shakespeare had to be careful not to make it too much or to disperse it and so confuse the conflict. In Cinthio, Iago's passion for Desdemona is a mainspring

---

[1]. So also with Princess Claribel, daughter of King Alonso of Naples, in *The Tempest*, and married to the King of Tunis, 'an African.' (II.1.119.)

of the action. In Shakespeare this is barely hinted at. The theme is transferred to Roderigo, so that Iago's motive is concentrated, and also that in the very opening of the play we learn his true character and are not deceived as Othello was.

It emerges in the first scene that Iago hates Othello. His pride and his reputation as a soldier have been wounded to the quick by his own general whom he has long served. His great services have been ignored and slighted. He is bent on revenge, both on Othello and on his supplanter Cassio. And not without reason. He is a proud professional soldier, of greater experience in war than Cassio. He is the fighting man who finds a chair-borne soldier promoted over his head. And presently Cassio cuts a pretty poor figure in his high office. Moreover, Iago is a Venetian, while Othello is a Moor, and Cassio a Florentine, both foreigners. He begins at once, with the help of Roderigo, on his first plot. And Othello has not yet appeared on the stage. We are clearly engaged upon a revenge-play.

The theme of reputation looms large in the play throughout, as it loomed large in the thoughts and passions of all Elizabethan Englishmen. The Earl of Essex would have understood Iago's feelings, which drove him into rebellion against the Queen. It was in no small degree this idol of reputation that helped to put Othello at Iago's mercy. Iago's first appeal to Othello's passions is by a threat to his 'good name,' the 'immediate jewel of the souls' of man or woman. Othello's remedy, like Iago's, is revenge for the loss of reputation. So Cassio, a soldier too, mourns his wounded reputation, 'the immortal part of himself.' In Othello's very last speech, like Prince Hamlet in his death-throes,

Othello makes his claim to honourable memory as he draws his sword to slay himself. It is strange indeed that Iago's famous speech deriding reputation to Cassio has been taken as if it were a soliloquy and the expression of his inmost thoughts.[1] There is deep and bitter irony in it, as well as mockery. Reputation is indeed 'oft got without merit,' as by Cassio, and 'lost without deserving,' as by Iago himself. Iago is no Falstaff.

As for the theme of sexual jealousy, so much harped upon in comment on the play, it actually first appears in Iago, and not in Othello, in the very first act, when he betrays jealousy of Othello, in terms of reputation again. 'It is thought abroad,' he says in a soliloquy, that his suspicions of Othello with Emilia are well-founded. And it adds to his burning desire for revenge upon Othello. So further, when he also suspects Cassio with Emilia. Is it going too far to speak of Iago as being 'perplexed in the extreme,' no less than Othello? No interpretation of this great tragedy of revenge and no representation of it upon the stage, can be less true to its significance than the conception of Iago as a passionless, calculating incarnation of the spirit of evil mastering the fates of men and women. Iago is driven by passion. His plots drive him, rather than are driven by him. He is driven to seeing that Roderigo must die, that Cassio must die, and finally that Emilia must be silenced or all is lost. Thinking himself to be master of his fate, he is yet driven by fate. He never dreamed that he would be landed into a fight for his own life. And in the end he is defeated, and knows it. Master of

---

1. He speaks to Othello of 'good name' in exactly the opposite sense

words, arguments, and suggestions, and of nothing else, Iago is silenced utterly:

From this time forth I never will speak word.

The truth is that Othello's judgment was not at fault in rejecting Iago as his lieutenant, as deputy for the general in his absence. Iago was no general, though an admirable fighting captain; a good man in a tight corner, but too apt to get into tight corners.

The conflict between Othello and Iago thus takes the form of a revenge-plot whereby Iago seeks to injure Othello by an attack upon the weakest and most sensitive quarter of his defences, and in such a way as to involve his other enemy Cassio in grave injury. Revenge, as Bacon wrote, is wild justice, and Iago could seek recourse to no other redress for his wrongs. In the course of that revenge, he succeeded so far that he led Othello into the same anarchic course of action, into the assumption of the office of righting wrongs done to him by Desdemona. Offended as they were in their private lives, they took upon themselves the execution of private justice upon the offenders. It cannot be doubted that Shakespeare was well aware, here as in *Hamlet*, of the significance of this aspect of his play, and that it loomed large in the reflection of his thought upon the problems it presented in the presence of these two usurping justicers.

Historians of the Elizabethan drama have too readily thought of the Revenge Tragedy as a literary fashion, and too little of its significance as a reflection of the Elizabethan life out of which it arose. The centralisation in the Crown of power and justice by the Tudor dynasty, an immense and gradual achievement, sought to eliminate the power of local magnates to exercise private justice within their own regions. The much abused and misunderstood Court of Star Chamber was set up by Henry the Seventh mainly to control, by the power of the Crown, this and other corruptions of justice, often indistinguishable from vengeance. We may recall the Physician in *Macbeth* whose art did not suffice to cure Lady Macbeth:

> Were I from Dunsinane away, and clear,
> Profit itself should hardly draw me here.

A provincial sufferer of wealth, calling a London physician, Dr. Story, into the country to attend to him, and dissatisfied with the failure of his skill, thrust him into his private dungeon in punishment for his incompetence. The famous William Clowes, more skilful or more fortunate, succeeded where Story failed, and was richly rewarded. George, Earl of Shrewsbury, at the command of Queen Elizabeth, kept Mary Queen of Scots in safe custody at Sheffield Castle. But she was followed as a prisoner there by Eleanor Breton under his son Gilbert, Earl of Shrewsbury, who revenged himself thus upon his father's mistress, and also by the confiscation of lands and properties legally conveyed to her. George, Earl of Cumberland, coveting the lands of a Yorkshire yeoman, sent his horsemen to bring him prisoner to Skipton Castle, and so to reduce him to reason. The suborning and bribing of juries, and their intimidation by the great, shook the King's justice in the counties. The records of the Courts of Star Chamber and of Chancery, from which these instances are cited, are thickly strewn with such exercises of private justice in all parts of England. There could be little doubt that in Shakespeare's Stratford Sir Thomas Lucy would be an ill man to cross. A Justice of the Peace might well confuse public with private justice in his function. It is significant indeed that Shakespeare in this play will have no truck with the fashionable moral anarchy which we find reflected in Chapman's revenge tragedies, and which exalts the law of private justice.

> Who to himself is law, no law doth need,
> Offends no law, and is a king indeed.

So says Bussy d'Ambois, who claims, by the right of reputation, to 'do a justice that exceeds the law.' Man was created free, and 'a free man's eminence' is above 'positive law.'

Two powerful streams of influence fought against submission to general or public justice under the Crown. The law of reputation, activated by pride, vanity and ancient tradition, joined hands with the new and extreme moral individualism, the law of virtue which claimed supremacy for private judgment. We may well see both in operation in *Coriolanus,* a play in which Shakespeare holds the balance even and steady. Public justice, it is true, is there wielded by unworthy hands, by the Tribunes, who are themselves accused of the pride of power as well as just pride of office. And we may allow the protest of Coriolanus to Volumnia:

> Would you have me
> False to my nature? Rather say, I play
> The man I am. (III.2.)

But this comes too close to a more dangerous claim, that he should stand

> As if a man were author of himself
> And knew no other kin. (V.3.)

This attitude for Shakespeare is indeed the very heart of villainy. 'I am myself alone', is the key to Richard the Third as to Iago. So for Edmund in *King Lear*. Nature is his goddess, and law is only custom. This lonely self-sufficiency, solitary even in the friendly company of other men, goes along with a secretiveness which marks the villain off from the normal exchange and communication of thought. Shakespeare's villains use words to conceal thought, such men as Bacon describes in his essay upon 'Dissimulation', the opposite at all points to the frank, emotional, rhetorical expansiveness of the Elizabethan Englishman. All we know about Shakespeare himself points to his friendly communicativeness with other men, and it is not with his approval that his Don John in *Much Ado About Nothing* boasts of his taciturnity: 'I am not of many words'.

In the end, Coriolanus abandons the private law by which he lives, and bends before a higher law that he cannot deny, in the crisis to which the law of reputation and virtue has brought him. He dies a victim to that same private law and justice at the hands of Aufidius. The circle is completed. We are left free to judge, except that we may not question the 'noble memory' that lives after him, with Aufidius himself as chief witness to his nobility.

The pitfall into which Othello fell was, however, more complex. Iago had no illusions about the motives of his own actions, and did not attempt to disguise them to himself. Othello's first explosion of decision is no less frank, when he calls up 'black vengeance from the hollow hell' and devotes himself to 'a capable and wide revenge.' But in the very act and word he invokes heaven also to register his sacred vow to effect this purpose. Again and again he invokes heaven as witness to Desdemona's falseness. In the dreadful scene of the execution of this vow there is an unmistakably hieratic approach to his fatal deed. He moves to Desdemona's bed as a priest to the altar. He even uses the word 'sacrifice' to define the spirit in which he comes to his act. It is in this spirit that he invites his victim to make her confession, to reconcile herself with God, and to seek his grace. He has gone much further than merely to make himself the instrument of human justice and her temporal sword, which Desdemona's sweetness tempts him to break. In the appalling confusion of his thought he has also identified himself with divine justice, intervening through him, a visitation of God's wrath upon Desdemona. I can attach no clear and certain significance to his word 'sacrifice' other than this sacramental sense, blasphemous though it be. The victim upon his altar, if in a state of penitence, will be taken by God to his mercy, in this priestlike act. It is Desdemona, recalcitrant and obstinate in her sin, who degrades it into murder.

The proof of Desdemona's innocence tears out of Othello's hands his sword of justice, and strips from him his imagined vestment of sacrifice, and all rags and tatters of illusion. His deed was not a deed 'worthy heaven,' to use that strange phrase of Emilia's which hints at an understanding of Othello's approach to his task. It damned him beneath all depth in hell. There is something of an appeal to true divine justice upon Iago in Othello's outraged cry:

> Are there no stones in heaven but what serves for the thunder?

But he is sure where he himself stands. He awaits his eternal judgment, and anticipates in vivid imagination the pains of hell to which he is destined. As for his judgment on earth, he has passed verdict upon himself, and retains execution also in his own hands. The word 'suicide' has prejudicial associations, and is ill fitted to his final act, so often commented on as an evasion of justice. On the contrary, it is Othello's own concluding act of justice. Until Lodovico speaks at this last moment, Othello still holds power and command in Cyprus. Driven by honour in all things, as he himself pleads—his only plea—he exercises his office a little longer, and public and private justice combine as he turns them now upon himself, rejecting all such mitigation and mercy as might have moved the Venetian state which he has served so well.

This final act, indeed, is the incontrovertible evidence of that return of Othello to heroic stature which is the main factor in the peace of mind, even the quiet exultation, which the end of the play leaves with us. The craft and subtlety of the devil or man have been brought to nought to human judgment at least, as we know when we lift our eyes from the cockpit of Cyprus, leaving Iago a ruined gambler in chains. He has failed to destroy Othello. It is left to Iago's other opponent, Cassio, to assure us that Othello's honour and reputation are safe. 'For he was great of heart.' He has failed to destroy love. For Desdemona remains to the end 'an ever-fixed mark' that alters not when it alteration finds, her love unconquerable, reaching out beyond death to the eclipsed sun of Othello's love, now radiant again and for ever. The shadow has passed too from the sun of Justice, eclipsed by the usurpation of the passions of hate and revenge arrogating her functions into private execution. There remains divine justice:

> And how his audit stands who knows save heaven?
> But in our circumstance and course of thought
> 'Tis heavy with him.

So Hamlet thought of his dead father, and so we must think of Othello and with better reason. Shakespeare does not spare us the vision of Othello's damnation, from Othello's own mouth. Why is it that we are not more oppressed, at the end of this play, by this vision of judgment? It is in sharp contrast with the vision that Shakespeare presents, in the mouth of Horatio, of Hamlet sung home to his rest by flights of angels. These are not our comments upon the action, they are from Shakespeare's pen, and the thoughts come from his mind, not ours. Are we content to know with Hamlet that we cannot audit the account here, and that the verdicts of divine justice are inscrutable? I do not think that we merely slide over the question, weakly hoping for the best, as a pacification of the tragic pity and fear that have been aroused within us.

Indeed it may seem that we come close to the Elizabethan passion for the vindication of honour and reputation which may lead the best men into strange vagaries, but yet remain the Pole-star by which they guide their sailing over the seas of life. This was the sea-mark of Coriolanus too, not pride as some are pleased to define it in assessing his admitted greatness. It seems very notable to me that in Greek tragedy the Chorus is apt to be insistent upon prudence and caution, with the common, general inclination to play safe, which is alien to the spirit of superior virtue in mankind. With the Greeks, the inscrutable, capricious gods are something of an occupational risk for the man of superior virtue. But in the universe of Christian Europe the tragic view of human life is in the main isolated from the theological view, which is beyond man's scrutiny. *Permitte divis cetera* is not necessarily an epicurean resignation. From this shipwreck of a galleon that set forth so gallantly there is triumphal salvage of merchandise of man's own lading, death contemned, a mind unconquered, and undefeated love.

Surely it is in these terms that we may say with Job, 'when men are cast down, then thou shalt say there is lifting up.'

The dilemma:
HAMLET

The tragedy of *Hamlet* has long been, for the critic as well as for the actor, a diploma-piece, and it cannot be approached without trepidation. Salutary warnings are not wanting. 'I shall find nothing new to say regarding either Shakespeare's drama or its hero, for everything has been said already — everything, and more than everything.' These are the words of the famous French critic Jules Lemaître, and they were written in 1886. They may now be read with a rueful smile, for since they were written a cataract of writing, in ever-increasing volume, and over a life-time of another seventy years, has poured over this critical precipice into an illimitable, troubled pool below.

In the vast scope and variety of this continuous comment, it may seem that a question of only minor interest to the commentators has been the intention of William Shakespeare in writing the play, or what he at least thought to be his intention. There is something of a conspiracy to reject whatever on the surface appears to be that intention in favour of a more recondite interpretation of the play as it affects us to-day. Simplicity of interpretation is suspect on the ground of its simplicity, though drama cannot live and move in obscurity. So the inclination of modern criticism is to seek above all alternative interpretations of action, character, and motive, beyond whatever was apparent in the play as it presented itself to its Elizabethan audience, as indeed to its modern audience and readers of the common sort.

Thus we are instructed that whatever delayed Hamlet's vengeance upon Claudius, it was not his desire to be assured, by certainty of the Ghost's evidence, or by the redoubled certainty of the Play scene, that there was just cause for vengeance. It is urged that such a motive was inconsistent with the character of Hamlet, a man of urbane intellectuality, and immune from such crude passions. He is a man, indeed, to be recognised as of our own modern stamp, and, as such, subject to psychological complexities familiar to us in Freudian analysis of behaviour. An Oedipus Complex is, in fact, looked upon as preferable to the long-standing diagnosis of Hamlet's constitutional inability to take decisions, though this diagnosis, however unacceptable, can at least be supported by some of the patient's own evidence in soliloquy.

The impact upon modern minds of this tremendous work of art is indeed so powerful that it is difficult to evade two critical pitfalls in our response to it and in our interpretation of its appeal to the world of to-day. A. C. Bradley has been generally blamed, not without reason, for expounding life and character in the tragedies of Shakespeare as if they were part of real life beyond the bounds of the play. It is an insidious temptation to commune with such a person as Hamlet as if he walked in the daylight, available for interview, in a new Garrick Jubilee procession. And there is something of a revival of an ancient heresy in approaching Shakespeare as the mysterious voice of Nature itself still waiting for decipherments beyond his own ken but discoverable to-day. But we may not lightly place such limits upon the awareness of the greatest dramatist in the world's history of the significance of his own creative work.

Professor C. H. Herford, as far back as in 1923, drew the dividing line in Shakespearean criticism between the approach of 'practical sagacity' and the approach of 'imaginative intuition.' It is perhaps of importance that the former, resting upon knowledge and observation, may reasonably hope, and has for its object, to convince by argument. It is the instrument so powerfully wielded by Dr. Johnson, and in our own century by the great American scholar G. L. Kittredge who formed a generation of opinion by his teaching, not least upon *Hamlet*, even more perhaps than by his writings, though he wrote decisively too. The latter, a more individual and personal approach, may hope at best to persuade or allure, but in the main is not concerned with seeking assent, being content with the appreciation proper to creative art. We can hardly deny the value of such an approach by gifted and sensitive modern minds, especially to a poetic dramatist of such insight and variety as Shakespeare, whose material is human nature and its complexities. But it may be that the resources of practical sagacity, in Herford's phrase, have not yet been exhausted, even in relation to *Hamlet*.

It has long been understood, of course, that the apparent problem facing Hamlet in the play is the question of the guilt of Claudius and consequently of his duty to avenge the wrong done, upon conviction by evidence. It cannot reasonably be doubted that this was the problem which the play was intended by Shakespeare to represent, and which its first actors and audiences accepted as the theme of the tragedy. But the dramatist, in his creation of the characters involved in this action, especially of its hero, Hamlet, went far beyond the bare bones of so simple a plot.

'He thinks only on men,' wrote Dr. Johnson, who was deeply concerned with the moral significance of the plays and their characters. Shakespeare thinks on whole men, not on types or formulae, men with their flesh and blood, their thoughts and passions, their strengths and weaknesses — sometimes beyond the needs of his plot and even with some irrelevance to its main course of action, as with Shylock and Malvolio— their setting in the small world of their own time, place, and society, in the greater world of humanity, and in the greatest world of the universe ruled by divine power and wisdom. With the true dramatist of Shakespeare's way of creation, each man on whom he thinks is unique. Certainly then, the study of Hamlet's character is all-important in the study of the play, as with the heroes of the other tragedies. It thus became possible, perhaps in Shakespeare's own time, and certainly in later ages, to complicate the problem of the play by considering Hamlet's temperament as an essential and decisive factor in the dramatic conflict upon which the play rests, even to make this factor usurp upon the apparent problem and transcend it. The play is thus brought into harmony with the concept of that *hamartia* leading to tragic catastrophe which the Renaissance had deduced from Aristotle after its fashion, and which the modern world has gratefully applied to Shakespeare's tragedy as a clue to his mysteries. Such an interpretation has recently been stated to be the explicit key to *Hamlet* as it appears in Olivier's film-version, 'the tragedy of a man who cannot make up his mind,' not for want of evidence, but because of a constitutional defect of character.

We cannot well resist this general approach to the much debated question of Hamlet's delays, if properly stated. It is a fact that in the elaboration of the character of Hamlet in this play, in this full-length picture of moral and philosophical perplexity and intellectual curiosity, there is in a certain sense a true delaying force in the action, and within this is enclosed all that may be said about the specific problems before him. Simplify Hamlet's character, and reduce his intellectual equipment, and the revenge-story would be told rapidly enough. But it would not then be Shakespeare's play. Orestes in Aeschylus makes no enquiry into the validity of the oracle of Apollo; he accepts it. But Hamlet, confronted by something like oracular guidance, is by his nature obliged to apply his mind to it. We do not normally, in the pursuit of justice or of scientific truth, consider procrastination as the only alternative to leaping to conclusions, a defect of the will as the only alternative to a defect of the intellect. And there was much to give Hamlet or any man pause even beyond the examination of evidence.

The capital evidence for setting up such a flaw in Hamlet's character as a key to the tragedy is contained in a well known speech (Act I.Sc. 4. ll. 23-38) which is used as a Prologue to Sir Laurence Olivier's film-version. This 'dram of eale' speech, however, obviously carried no such significance to Shakespeare or to his company of actors. It is to be found in the Second Quarto of the play, printed in 1604 from Shakespeare's manuscript. But in the Folio edition it is not to be found. It is universally agreed that the Folio text derives from the prompt-copy used in the performance of the play. The speech was in fact cut in the course of adaptation for the stage. It is impossible to believe that a key-speech could thus be dispensed with in actual production, if key-speech it were. But plainly it was not so in the eyes of Shakespeare who wrote the play, or of Burbage who created the part of Hamlet.

To make it imperative to accept Hamlet's delays as a moral weakness, it seems reasonable to presume that the normal reasons for the postponement of decision and action are wanting, or are inadequate, and that no true or cogent dilemma was in fact presented to Hamlet for his resolution.

We may well at this stage recall Hamlet's last words, or almost his last words, spoken to Horatio, his heart's companion, words which have evoked much comment, like everything else in the play.

> O God, Horatio, what a wounded name,
> Things standing thus unknown, shall live behind me.

> If thou didst ever hold me in thy heart,
> Absent thee from felicity awhile,
> And in this harsh world draw thy breath in pain,
> To tell my story.

He has already once bidden Horatio to

> report me and my cause aright
> To the unsatisfied.

And finally, with his dying voice nominating Fortinbras to succeed him as rightful king, for the *third* time he charges Horatio to explain to Fortinbras the course he took. It would be merely ludicrous to imagine that what Horatio was to tell the world, and to tell Fortinbras, was that Hamlet was to be excused for not being able to make up his mind sooner. Yet no character in fiction has examined the workings of his own mind more narrowly, and we may not airily assume naïveté or self-deception in this rich endowment of a complex person. What the world was to be told was a matter of greater weight than this, and I do not recall that the answer to this question has yet been fully given. It may perhaps help us to interpret his anxiety if we consider it as a problem of justice.

It is customary to describe *Hamlet* as a Revenge-Tragedy. It is less frequently realized how closely vengeance and justice are allied in men's thoughts, though Bacon's definition of revenge as 'wild justice' is now proverbial. And when we quote the sentence, 'Vengeance is mine, saith the Lord,' we can hardly imagine that vengeance here means anything but divine justice supreme in the universe. In Greek tragedy the dividing-line is narrow between the judge and the avenger, the δικαστής and the δικηφόρος, the dispenser of justice and the instrument of justice. Upon Electra's enquiry in the *Choephorae*, the Chorus indeed rejects such hair-splitting in favour of the simple *lex talionis*, life exacted in payment for life, whatever the instrument. But Electra, like Hamlet, requires to be reassured that such vengeance would indeed be the will of Heaven. And Orestes, in the same play, reports the command of Apollo laid upon him to avenge his father Agamemnon upon his slayer Aegisthus.

The theme of justice in vengeance recurs again and again in Shakespeare as elsewhere. It is a most significant difference between the revenge sought by Iago, and that executed by Othello, that Iago makes no pretence to be the instrument of a higher justice. His motives are plainly those recognised by contemporary theology as arising out of the deadly sin of envy. But Othello, moved as he too is by personal wrongs, above all to the Elizabethan demi-god of reputation, is yet upheld by the belief that it is laid upon him to do God's will upon a source of evil, the more perilous for its beauty. In *Julius Caesar*, Brutus uses the same image of a sacrifice which Othello invokes, to justify the slaying of Caesar, and Antony at the end distinguishes him honourably from the others who were moved only by envy. Yet Antony is careful in his speeches to the citizens to cancel out Brutus' explicit claim to them that Caesar died for his offences to Rome, by attributing to all the conspirators the lower motive of 'private griefs,' not justice. This was, beyond reasonable doubt, part of Hamlet's anxiety throughout the play, and especially at the end, lest another Antony arise to condemn his actions as dictated by motives of private vengeance. 'There's something rotten in the state of Denmark,' and 'The time is out of joint,' these are fundamental among Hamlet's concerns and among his motives.

It is plainly evident from Shakespeare's references to Julius Caesar and his story, elsewhere than in the tragedy devoted to them, and more than once in *Hamlet,* how they haunted Shakespeare's imagination, as indeed that of all Christendom. A strong tradition of the medieval world saw it as the supreme betrayal, and Brutus as the supreme traitor, fit to share with Satan the deepest pit in Dante's Inferno. The Renaissance changed the balance of thought, it is true. But Shakespeare does not cast Caesar to the wolves, and Caesar's faults in his play serve mainly to make the conspiracy credible and tolerable. The action ends with the downfall of the conspirators and the triumph of the dead Caesar over his enemies. Yet there is no verdict to be found in Shakespeare's play, and Brutus takes the honours at the end. The balance of justice hangs even in a conflict of virtues.

In all probability Shakespeare moved directly from *Julius Caesar* to the composition of *Hamlet,* or at least with no great interval, and with the problems of *Julius Caesar* still in his mind. It is no mere coincidence that Polonius recalls to Hamlet his own performance as an amateur actor of the part of Julius Caesar.

Ham. My lord, you played once i' th' university, you say?
Pol. That did I, my lord, and was accounted a good actor.
Ham. What did you enact?

Pol. I did enact Julius Caesar. I was killed i' th' Capitol, Brutus killed me.
Ham. It was a brute part of him to kill so capital a calf there.

The combination of academic pursuits with an active and practical interest in stage and drama is of ancient standing at Oxford and Cambridge, where in present days too we are familiar with the participation of Fellows and undergraduates in dramatic performances, though the original close relation of such exercises with a classical education is now for the most part forgotten. This collaboration is reflected in the casts recorded in surviving manuscript plays of the Elizabethan period at both Universities. The passage from *Hamlet* is therefore a reference to a feature of University life which was well known to the professional actors, as we may see here or in the Cambridge academic play *The Return from Parnassus*. Like that play, it may seem to reflect the somewhat critical attitude of the professionals towards the amateur stage and the amateur expert. We may well be led to think even that the passage has autobiographical significance. Shakespeare and his fellows surely were acquainted with the approach of lovers of the stage and drama who entertained them with reminiscences beginning, 'When I was up at Oxford.' Certainly we know that even the nobility did not disdain the friendship of an outstanding actor like Burbage. It is tempting indeed to surmise that one such patron of the London stage recalled to Shakespeare his own student performance in a play produced at Christ Church in Oxford some twenty years before *Hamlet* was written.[1] The play was in Latin, *Caesar Interfectus*, 'The Killing of Caesar,' by Dr. Richard Eedes, to whom Meres alludes in 1598 as among 'our best for Tragedie.' It was probably performed in February, 1582. Only the Epilogue to this play survives in a Bodleian manuscript. Had the whole play survived, with the usual cast of College actors, it would have been most exciting to pursue their careers in the hope of finding a possible candidate for the honour of sitting to Shakespeare for the part of Polonius. He may even have offered guidance to the company upon the writing and acting of *Julius Caesar* a year or two before. And it is surely conceivable that Shakespeare took his mild revenge upon a bore, who very possibly, like Polonius, was now in high office at Court, by turning him into Polonius in this scene. Polonius, it will be observed, is also a dramatic critic of the academic sort, as against the very practical approach of Hamlet and the actors themselves to their art.

We should not, however, treat these passages in *Hamlet* upon the art of acting as a mere excursus or irrelevancy, as they are often treated. The dramatic situation justifies them fully, as necessary to the cause and purpose of the action. It is all-important to Hamlet that the Players should be fit instruments for his design, that the acting of the play should be realistic and natural, so that Claudius may see himself in the mirror of nature, and betray himself. And the audience

---

1. It is extremely improbable that Shakespeare's reference is to the much later Trinity College, Oxford, play in English, *The Tragedie of Caesar and Pompey*, or *Caesar's Revenge*, printed in 1606. In this play, we observe, Caesar is not 'killed i' the Capitol' but in the Campus Martius, the *curia Pompeii*, in agreement with authentic history. Its date is uncertain, and it might even be later than *Hamlet* in origin.

III: THE DILEMMA [62]

should be led to anticipate the success of the device. It is no mere question of abstract criteria of histrionic or dramatic art. Can we wonder that the Prince labours the point with his travelling actors, even if we consider only the immediate needs of the action? It was desperately necessary not only for Hamlet to be certain, but for his certainty to be shared if possible by others in Denmark and at the Court, by the spectacle of something like ocular proof, something like a public confession of guilt by the King. Here was something that Horatio in due course could report aright. In the meantime the decision is taken, and war is declared between Hamlet and Claudius. Claudius too has taken his decision.

It is well to recall that, throughout, Hamlet must think and act alone, in his appalling responsibility. He cannot lead the nation to revolt. As Brutus found the Roman mob an easily breakable reed, so Hamlet had nothing to hope for in the Danish mob, though they love him well enough to give Claudius pause in thoughts of overt attack upon him. They are irresponsible, roused to sudden fury by Laertes and as soon quelled and cowed. They are indeed an English mob, not the *plebs* of Rome who have so powerful a corporate personality in *Julius Caesar* and in *Coriolanus*. They are little more than 'noises off,' or almost 'off.' Hamlet must cut himself off even from his closest friend Horatio in the secrecy of his decisions. And his dedicated life can no longer make room for his beloved Ophelia, lest she be drawn into the whirlpool. All causes must give way save the supreme cause. And Hamlet's feigned madness, setting him apart from all men, is the reflection of his ultimate and desperate solitariness in his grievous fate, a refuge as also a device.

What Hamlet has to decide about is murder, and murder of a king at that, his own uncle, and husband of his own mother. Some considerable degree of hesitation is natural in the commission of murder, still more of regicide. Macbeth has terrible qualms, and only a shag-eared murderer can go to it as to the manner born. Unhesitating immediate decision in a trial at law is no merit in itself in the judge who tries it, or in the jury which returns a verdict. Hamlet is much more in the position of a judge in a trial of Claudius than we are apt to realize. And he is sitting without a jury.

There was no alternative to murder, for Hamlet as for Brutus in that great play which marked Shakespeare's turning to tragedy. In neither case is deposition even considered as a possible remedy for the situation, and for good reason in Elizabethan England, when the theme of deposition of a reigning monarch was political dynamite, more perilous than regicide, especially in Elizabeth's late years. The Deposition Scene in *Richard the Second*, as all know, was censored and deleted from the first Quarto edition of the play in 1597. The revival of the play was associated with the conspiracy of the Earl of Essex in 1600. And *Hamlet* was written and first acted between 1598 and 1600. The cruel decision before Hamlet was apparently murder or nothing.

The dilemma facing him was familiar in Elizabethan thought upon problems of justice, familiar to Shakespeare also and to his audience. We may see it plainly set forth in the writings of William Perkins, for example, a practical theologian who had become something of a country-wide court of appeal for public opinion, and whose influence was recognised, and satirised, in a controversy at Stratford upon the appointment of a new Vicar there. Bloodshed cries aloud for vengeance, and cannot be silenced until blood is shed in return by justice. Yet the Prince is above justice, for there is no judge to pass judgment upon him, none in a superior place to wield justice against him. Evil-doing in a king must be borne patiently, for he is subject only to God. It is thus that Perkins states the problem. It is well to recall that this is the doctrine of one accused in his own day, and since, of standing for Puritan Nonconformity. King Charles could well have appealed to such authority also, and not only, as we are led to think by Whig historians, to new and unfamiliar conceptions of the monarchy in England.

The problem was familiar in Greek tragedy, and was crystallized in a stark phrase in the *Prometheus Bound* of Aeschylus. 'Only the tyrant is free.' The ruler is exempt, where all others are subject to justice. There is a monumental passage in Fletcher's tragedy, *Valentinian*, after the Emperor Valentinian has forced to his evil will the chaste Lucina, wife of his General Maximus.

> *Lucina*   As long as there is motion in my body
> And life to give me words, I'll cry for justice.
> *Valentinian* Justice shall never hear ye, *I am justice.*

There remains only a tortuous path of vengeance by Maximus, not in his own person, by devices to overcome the insuperable obstacle that halts justice before a king. It was infinitely more difficult for Hamlet.

He was called upon to set right something rotten in the State of Denmark. He could neither shirk nor delegate his task, but must execute it himself. The core of the rottenness was his uncle Claudius, King of Denmark, linked with his mother Gertrude in unholy marriage. And she was the Queen. Claudius was legally no usurper, but King by election after the Danish fashion, and a King of power and quality, worthy of his throne. Both were hedged around with that divinity which is the appanage of crowned and anointed King and Queen. How could justice be invoked against them, even upon certainty of blood crying for vengeance?

There is awareness of this dilemma even in the mind of Claudius, as appears in the Prayer scene, in that moment of self-revelation. He is possessed of the effects for which he murdered his brother, and one of these effects is immunity from justice, as is implicit in the words:

> Offence's gilded hand may shove by justice,
> And oft 'tis seen the wicked prize itself
> Buys out the law.

Justice, that is to say, other than the final judgment of the soul, in which there is no shuffling. The Prayer scene, be it remembered, follows immediately upon the full statement by Rosencrantz of the significance in the commonwealth of the life of its Prince. In Fletcher, it is put into the mouth of the noblest and most honoured citizen of Rome, the soldier Aecius, not a flatterer of emperors. And presently Claudius faces the desperate Laertes calmly, not only with courage but with the assurance of divine protection for his royalty.

How then was Hamlet to emerge from such a dilemma with the certainty he needed before entering upon so dire an action? He had first to assure himself of just grounds for action, in the preliminary dilemma presented by the nature of his evidence, the very cogent and dreadful danger of diabolical instigation using the mask of his dead father's ghost to seduce him to evil. Not until the Play scene is he confirmed in knowledge that the truth has thus been revealed to him. But there is more in it. With this knowledge comes conviction that there has been an intervention of divine will and purpose in this revelation addressed to him.

The play of *Hamlet* is generally considered and described as a Revenge Tragedy, and is seen as one of a series of such tragedies beginning with Kyd's *Spanish Tragedy*. But *Hamlet* does not fit into the pattern of pure revenge, into the Italian world of Verona, of Tybalt and Mercutio, and of Shakespeare's England too, of gentleman and nobleman with his rapier by his side to defend his honour, to revenge any slight upon it by instant brawl or by formal duel. In such a world, graves and vaults held innumerable men who having had honour died 'a Wednesday, men bearded like the pard,

Jealous in honour, sudden and quick in quarrel.

It was a world of individualists, vindicating themselves by their own personality and their own powers, a world torn by conflicting individuals concerned with their reputations. To such anarchy the Tudor conception of an ordered society controlled at the centre, the Prince, the fountain of honour as of justice, was unalterably opposed. The passion of revenge was universally condemned. For the religious thinker the justice of God must be left to work divine will, and we for our part should forgive our enemies. Or if we cannot rise to this Christian height, then we must seek our remedy of the magistrates, who are under the King, who is under God. Hamlet, as true Prince and true man, could not be

Jealous in honour, sudden and quick in quarrel,

not in his major quarrel. He was of Romeo's mind, who went to extremes to avoid a duel with Tybalt. Mercutio's death in such a fight is a condemnation of the violent settling of quarrels. And where Hamlet, caught by surprise and off his guard, *is* sudden and quick, in his killing of the unseen, unknown Polonius behind the arras, the consequences are disastrous and unmeasured. His refusal to kill Claudius in the Prayer scene is an outstanding example of Hamlet's deliberate conscience ruling him, below the surface of the motives with which he cloaks it. Claudius bids Laertes execute his threat to cut Hamlet's throat in the church if necessary.

King No place indeed should murder sanctuarize.
    Revenge should have no bounds. (IV. 7. 126-7.)

Here lies the deep gulf fixed between a Claudius and a Hamlet. And here is the true significance of Hamlet's action and words in the Prayer scene. The King is in sanctuary, as Hamlet's words make clear, though their emphasis lies upon the theme of complete vengeance. There divinity truly hedges Claudius from death. To kill him now would be sacrilege. And if at any moment there is room for sympathy with Claudius, as in this torment of his soul, it is more than counterbalanced by the sharp irony of his words to Laertes, after Hamlet has spared *his* life in the sanctuary of prayer.

Conscience indeed makes a coward of Hamlet, if it is cowardice to seek not only certainty of knowledge but certainty also of his right and duty to execute justice. The spectacle presented by the play is thus the long and necessarily slow process of the acquisition of those certainties. We see the gradual arrival of Hamlet at the solution of his dilemma in the execution of justice. He does not at first question the status of Claudius as King, even if he had popped in between the election and Hamlet's own hopes, and even if he were a satyr to the Hyperion of the old King. Hamlet would not dream of moving to assert his own claims, his own ambition. He can only move as an instrument of divine justice. Conviction of his duty grows along with conviction that Claudius is not true King in the eyes of Heaven, that a higher sanction invalidates his election. After the Play scene, Hamlet is ready to 'take the Ghost's word for a thousand pounds.' And part of the Ghost's word is that he has permission from on high to carry out his mission to Hamlet, to command Hamlet to purge Denmark and to avenge the shedding of royal blood. So Hamlet moves on in the Closet scene to the dismissal of Claudius as murderer and villain, 'a vice of kings, a cutpurse of the empire and the rule,' no true and complete King but 'a king of shreds and patches.' And with this comes the full assertion of the dread task of Heaven's justiciar that is laid upon him:

> Heaven hath pleased it so,
> To punish me with this, and this with me,
> That I must be their scourge and minister.[1]

When we next meet Hamlet we see more plainly still that he has deposed Claudius in his mind and indeed has assumed kingship himself. This is the meaning of the startling words he uses when he leaps into Ophelia's grave: 'This is I, Hamlet *the Dane*,' words which can bear no other significance in Elizabethan England. With them the dilemma vanishes.

The more importance we attach to the foundations of justice in Hamlet's thoughts and motives, the more fully we understand the apparent delays in his actions about which so much has been written and which do not appear in the reading or the acting of the play. We should have heard much less about these delays but for Hamlet's own single reference to them and the Ghost's querulous complaint. Shakespeare relates this old story of Hamlet's revenge to the English world of thought of his own time, and so interpreting it enriches and deepens his tragedy with the reflection of significances lively and active in the minds of men, such men as went to see his play acted, such a man as the writer himself of a play that was great beyond expectation from such a source.

It is only in a partial and hasty survey of the scene and atmosphere of this play that a shadow of self-absorption and egoism may be felt to be cast upon Hamlet's character by his insistent charge laid upon

See Appendix Note B on this passage.

Horatio to live on to report him and his cause aright. It is an unacceptable suggestion that it would have been more gracious for him to have less concern for his own reputation and a more humane and unselfish motive for the saving of Horatio's life. We are moving here in a world of greater and more complex nobility than in that Greek tragedy in which we may be tempted to find a parallel to Hamlet's dying command. In Sophocles' magnificent play, the last prayer of Ajax to Zeus desires that the god will send a messenger to report his suicide to Teucer, lest his body, dead in honour, fall a dishonoured prey to dogs and birds. For Ajax, death is the friend, the atonement, and purgation for dishonour, in the private accounts of a man of honour, who must die nobly, as the only alternative to living nobly.

> ἀλλ' ἢ καλῶς ζῆν ἢ καλῶς τεθνηκέναι
> τὸν εὐγενῆ χρή (*Ajax*, 479-480)

Such is not Hamlet's dilemma, but it is indeed Horatio's as Hamlet was well aware. Horatio's honour is at stake, and his own reputation. To survive Hamlet is shame in his eyes, even as Kent heard the voice of the dead Lear calling him to join him in death.

We are perhaps inclined by our modern outlook to envisage Horatio as Hamlet's equal as one gentleman with another, fellow-students and comrades. But Horatio's own view of his companionship with Hamlet is 'your poor servant ever,' in the words he uses on their first meeting in the play. For him Hamlet is 'my lord,' 'my honoured lord.' Hamlet *thou*'s Horatio, never Horatio Hamlet. Horatio, like Kent, was of one mind with Byrthnoth in *The Battle of Maldon*: 'I think to lay me down by the side of my lord.'

Roman honour and old English honour were at one on this, the Roman and Germanic bases of English life and virtue which animated Byrthnoth and his companions when the Prince had fallen in battle. A higher loyalty must therefore be invoked to overcome the impulse of the personal honour of the warrior-companion, and Hamlet appeals to this higher loyalty in significantly reiterated injunctions. Horatio must continue to serve his lord by living on. It is in fact the only argument that could have saved Horatio's life. It was also the argument that the old King used to his son Hamlet. 'If thou didst ever hold me in thy heart,' see that justice is done. 'If thou didst ever thy dear father love,' see that it is done upon the usurper. For Hamlet as for Horatio, the felicity of honourable suicide was forbidden finally by the call of duty.

The issues are greater than Hamlet's personal reputation, powerful as is this motive alone. The issues are the safety, honour, and welfare of Denmark, and the success or failure of Hamlet's sacrifice of himself to the cause laid upon him. Beyond even this is the vindication of justice as wrought by Hamlet, the Prince-King instrument of God's judgment. Justice must not only be done, but must be seen to be done. Only Horatio can ensure this in his report of the whole action 'to the yet unknowing world,' the more urgently 'even while men's minds are wild.' Hamlet's concern for justice dominates the play throughout. The issues are far greater than those of mere life and death, which loom so large in materialistic thought. The tragedies that set forth for us the nobler manifestations of the human spirit have for theme not the triumph of death but the conquest of death reduced to a negligible irrelevance where men rise to their full stature.

Shakespeare's Elizabethan audience would have no doubt upon the nature of the charge that the dying Hamlet laid upon Horatio to report him and his cause aright. They would enlarge upon it to each other after the play was done. It is not merely that Hamlet was no avenger of a personal wrong, not merely even that he was the servant of that Providence in which he shows his full trust throughout. It is that he was God's justiciar in Denmark as rightful successor in the eyes of Heaven to his murdered father, guided by heavenly intervention. He could therefore as true King perform the will of Heaven against a false king. Dying in his sacred office and duty, the sacrifice for God's justice in Denmark, flights of angels sing him to his rest and to his reward. This is Horatio's epitaph upon the dead Hamlet, for whom as for another pilgrim, at the end of his progress, the angels sang, and the trumpets sounded.

The quandary:
KING LEAR

If *Hamlet* is a diploma-piece for the literary critic as for the actor, *King Lear* is a work of dramatic art which reduces criticism to intellectual humility. It imposes itself upon the receptive mind and imagination with the submissive awe that is moved by the crash of thunder and the explosions of lightning among snow-clad Alpine peaks, or by the first vision through a powerful telescope of the ringed planet of Saturn in illimitable space. When Gustav Holst sought to reflect Saturn in music in his *Planets*, his mind was haunted by the colossal ancient figure of the Greek god with which Keats opened *Hyperion*, yet from that still monument he moved into the clash and clangour of the vast revolving rings which he heard breaking the music of the spheres in harsh dissonance. The intellec-

[74]

tual concept of age with which he began yielded to the pressure of more immediate, more powerful intuition in contemplation. The tumult yields to a deep, warm melody of love, which dies away into an infinity of silence. And the image of Shakespeare's *King Lear* comes unbidden to hover through the powerful music.

Certainly, with *King Lear*, the critic-interpreter, beaten down by that overwhelming disturbance of the emotions which Dr. Johnson recorded, finds his powers of intellectual abstraction superseded by the ceaseless renewal of the huge, tidal attraction of this planet of art upon the feelings and the soul. 'This tempest will not give me leave to ponder,' says Lear, and we are stunned as he was. Dr. Johnson was writing as an editor, forcing himself, as in duty bound, to detached textual considerations in revising the last scenes of the tragedy. No play offers equal difficulties to the textual editor, for other than those textual reasons to which in the main emotional responses are irrelevant. In the very act of considering the words and their possible variations, the editorial mind slips lightly out of gear, and more mysterious powers enter into possession in long and dreaming trains of thought and imagination.

> Pray you undo this button. Thank you sir.
> Do you see this? Look on her, look her lips—
> Look there, look there —

And upon these words Lear dies. There is some debate upon the question whose button is to be undone, and upon the significance of varying Quarto and Folio readings. But between the editor and his problems there intervenes the moving certainty that here we are watching Lear slip round the corner of this known world of time and space into a kind of fourth dimensional world, with a glimpse before he disappears of what he sees already around that corner of eternity, his beloved Cordelia awaiting him there, her lips smiling again for Lear.

Our modern minds are resistant to such a conception of the old King's death, and are apt at best to gratify him with a hallucination or an illusion. Yet for the Elizabethans, and for Shakespeare, the unseen other world of eternity was not only more certain in men's belief, but it was closer to the world of human reality, the dividing line more unstable, less sharply defined, with frequent traffic between the two worlds. A man prepared his baggage for his passage through death to that other world as he would prepare for a journey from Stratford to London, not booted and spurred, but shriven, anointed, having made his peace with God as well as his last will and testament, indeed as part of that peace. For so the Order for the Visitation of the Sick admonishes a man 'to make his Will . . . for the better discharging of his conscience.' Even Falstaff, we are told by Mrs. Quickly, 'made a finer end, and went away an it had been any Christom child.' The malefactor upon execution was sent to his account, not with his account irrevocably closed as in modern materialistic humanitarian thought. The next world was indeed only around the corner from this world, as all men knew. And Lear for long had 'but usurped his life,' as Kent tells us, already on the verge.

Drawing back with unwilling effort from such a spiritual and emotional intuition, the textual question finds the intellect affected, perhaps prejudiced. In the Quarto text of 1608 all we have of these three lines is the first, in the form

pray you undo this button, thank you sir. o.o.o.o.

And upon this series of groans, Lear dies. It was thus that the death of Lear was played by Christopher Simpson with his company in their repertory for 1609 on their long Yorkshire tour, on which they also played *Pericles,* having bought their Quarto play books from the wide choice available in the London bookshops. What are we then to say concerning the two crucial lines missing in the Quarto? We may not dismiss the Quarto text, for all its faults, as defective and devoid of authority. The Folio text indeed shows clear signs of abridgment and revision, and the Quarto text is our sole authority for some three hundred lines wanting in the Folio. It seems clear that these two lines were added during the later history of the play between 1608 and 1623, and we may well ask why in a general abridgment even a small addition was made. It is impossible to think the question insignificant in so highly wrought a play, or to believe that the lines were added only to accompany further stage-business with a mirror or a feather, after Lear's certainty of Cordelia's physical death, and after his words

Never, never, never, never, never.

Such an anticlimax would verge on the ludicrous. There is ground for conviction that Shakespeare added these lines deliberately, and with a far deeper intention. So we see Lear in death, broken certainly upon the rack of the tough world, but turning again home, love transcending death.

Nowhere, in the whole range of Shakespeare's work, is the desire so acutely felt as in *King Lear* to be able to consult Shakespeare himself upon the words he had written and upon their significance in his mind.

The desperate painfulness of the tragic ending of *King Lear* led the stage, when the brave Elizabethan days were past, to accept for almost two hundred years Tate's sentimentalized version with a happy ending, Lear surviving and Cordelia suitably married to Edgar. It is a rare, indeed an amiable, confession of weakness that led A. C. Bradley to wish that Shakespeare had saved Lear and Cordelia from the general wreck to enjoy peace and happiness together, though he is careful to insist that his wish rests upon principles of dramatic perfection, not upon sentiment. Yet never did Shakespeare take a more deliberate or a more striking decision than to reject version after version of the story, in Spenser, in Holinshed, or in the old play in which this happy ending closes an episode in British history. We may well feel that if there has been revulsion against Shakespeare's desperate conclusions here, no less instinctive and powerful was Shakespeare's revulsion against the epilogue to this happy ending in Holinshed, the renewal of civil war, the defeat of Cordelia Queen of Britain, and her death at her own hands. Shakespeare's story, at any rate, had a conclusion in which everything was concluded, and if Cordelia was hanged, she did not hang herself as in Holinshed.

There is no subject upon which Bradley is more guarded, and more inconclusive, than the question of poetical justice. Yet through a maze of words it would seem that his conception of dramatic principles, as applied to *King Lear,* is offended by the gross disproportion between cause and effect in the catastrophe of this tragedy. He agrees that we may not measure the consequences of flaws in character in precise proportion to their results, and the logic of tragedy is not the logic of justice. Yet for him, here in *King Lear,* the vast sway of moral equilibrium in the universe is wanting, and there is consequently aesthetic dissatisfaction. Bradley's dissatisfaction finds itself reflected in the not uncommon estimate of the play as a tragedy of pessimistic outlook upon the world of men, and undue stress is still frequently laid upon Gloucester's words:

> As flies to wanton boys, are we to the gods;
> They kill us for their sport.

Too much stress has certainly been laid on what is described as the fairy-tale basis of the story of *King Lear,* with a consequent tendency to interpret the play in terms of cloudy symbolism for want of problems of human reality. What King in his senses, it is argued, would in real life divide his kingdom among his three daughters, abdicate, and spend his days thereafter in rotation with each in turn? How could a drama of living men and women emerge from such a fanciful theme? The modern world indeed might come closer in reality to Lear's action, in the avoidance of destruction of an estate by death-duties, with the device of deeds of gift to children. But in Elizabethan days funeral expenses were a far greater tax upon an estate than the claims of the Exchequer. Admittedly, the story was history, and was fact, to Shakespeare and the Elizabethans. Holinshed tells it, with a portrait of King Lear himself, bearded and helmeted, and a revolting woodcut of Cordelia, to illustrate it. There are parallels in classical history, and indeed in the early Elizabethan drama, as in *Gorboduc*. But we may perhaps distinguish between history and fairy-tale legend.

What we cannot do, is to deny the evidence of recorded contemporary events that such actions, not by kings certainly, but by men of great estate, were of frequent occurrence in Shakespeare's time. Some bear unexpected resemblances to the story of Lear as Shakespeare tells it. There was, for example, the Yorkshireman Ralph Hansby, who divided his great estates among his three daughters upon their marriage. He had no son, and he abdicated his greatness to continue it only in the advancement of his daughters. Two of them were ungrateful, but the third was his Cordelia, who married Sir John York. The career of Lady Julian York, a steadfast, loyal, obstinate soul, may be followed in state records up to her long imprisonment by King James for recusancy. Cordelia, we may well hold, would have been a recusant, Catholic or Puritan, in Shakespeare's day, averse by her nature to commodious conformity, to her great loss. In the story of the life of Brian Annesley, it has been recorded that the name of the youngest of his three daughters was actually Cordelia.[1]

Closest of all in some respects is the story of Sir William Allen, a very wealthy old Londoner, about which there is the fullest detail in Chancery records, a very lamentable story indeed.[2] Sir William was for long a leading figure in the Company of Merchant Adventurers. He had his day of quasi-royalty, for he was

---

1. G. M. Young. 'Shakespeare and the Termers,' in *Proceedings of the British Academy* Vol. xxxiii. The Hansby-York material is unpublished.
2. P.R.O. C24/210/Verzelyn v Allen; C24/211/Allen v Verzelyn.

Lord Mayor of London, and was knighted by the Queen in his year of office, in 1571. He lived on to be over eighty years of age, and found his great possessions a heavy burden from which he desired relief. He had moreover found himself growing forgetful in his great old age.

> Methinks I should know you, and know this man,
> Yet I am doubtful. For I am mainly ignorant
> What place this is; and all the skill I have
> Remembers not these garments; nor I know not
> Where I did lodge last night.

Sir William had three daughters, all married, one of them to a Frenchman, Francis Verzelin. So he divided his great properties among the three daughters, and arranged that he should stay with each of them in turn, at one of the houses that had been his own. But once they had entered into possession, they treated him very ill, and grudged him all service and comfort. Being so very old a man, he felt the cold bitterly, and desired warmth. But his daughters, so the Court was told, 'limited his fire,' kept him short of wood and coal, and treated his childish querulous protests with scorn and disdain. Coal was very dear, they said, an unnecessary expense. So Goneril and Regan with Lear's knights. 'What need *one?*' said Regan, 'this house is little.'

> Dear daughter, I confess that I am old;
> Age is unnecessary, on my knees I beg
> That you'll vouchsafe me raiment, bed and food.

And he kneels to Regan. What could be said for these pelican daughters?

> *Goneril* His knights grow riotous, and himself
>   upbraids us

> On every trifle...
> You strike my people, and your disordered rabble
> Make servants of their betters.

So Sir William's daughters complained that he was rude to their servants, called them 'fussocks,' awkward, unhandy—surely very mild abuse.[1] So at last he died, in great misery, and died with a father's curse upon them. There was no Cordelia among these three.

Sir William probably was in truth an obstinate, self-willed old man, as indeed Lear was with perhaps more justification, by virtue of his kingship. Sir William had a wife, Lady Mary Allen, who possibly resisted in vain his dangerous decision. A mother knows her own daughters, and a woman is more practical-minded, more critical of ideas. Lear, it may be noted, has no Queen in the play to defend her own crown as well as his. Like Hansby and Allen, he also has no son. There was none of power to question his self-will in the solitary absoluteness of his royalty. We must not put from our consideration the part of truth in what Goneril and Regan have to say in their judgment of his character and of his action in the very first scene, even in the first flush of their rich succession.

> *Regan:* 'Tis the infirmity of his age; yet he hath *ever* but slenderly known himself.
>
> *Goneril:* The best and soundest of his time hath been but rash, then must we look from his age to receive not alone the imperfections of long-ingrafted condition, but therewithal the unruly waywardness that infirm and choleric years bring with them.

---

[1]. N.E.D. cites *fussock* as first occurring in the 18th century.

It is something more than a coincidence that the Lear story first emerged on the London stage soon after the great stir which the story of Sir William Allen made in London. The case occupied the Court of Chancery for a long time in 1588 to 1589, and the early play, *The True Chronicle History of King Leir*, upon which in some measure Shakespeare founded his great tragedy, followed perhaps a year later. It may well be that this first play was designed to take advantage of the reflection on the stage of a current *cause célèbre* in actual London life. At all events, it must be conceded that no Elizabethan would accept the dismissal of the preliminary action of the play as a fairy-tale theme, remote from actuality. We may reasonably believe that Shakespeare knew this story of Sir William and his daughters, for he was certainly in London at the time when it was the talk of the town. How, we may well ask, would this knowledge affect his treatment of the story of King Lear when he turned one day to this old play which was in print in 1605, and saw in it material for the supreme exercise of his tragic genius?

It is a far cry from a Christian merchant-knight of Shakespeare's London to a pagan King of Britain in that remote world in which history merges into legend. What could be common to these two, save the mere story? The knowledge of this contemporary affair would surely lend immediacy and poignancy to these figures from the ancient past, and to their problems, in the chronicled story of Holinshed, partially recreated in the old play. And it would help Shakespeare to penetrate to the common elements of human nature involved in such a story as it affected two such various sets of people and sets of facts. It would impel him, finally, to seek out some philosophic significance in which these events could be reconciled with the ultimate order and meaning of the universe of God and man, to arrive indeed at what we call tragic reconciliation.

The story of Sir William Allen is merely desperate, it would seem, and totally devoid of that measure of poetic justice which marks the story that came to Shakespeare from Holinshed. There he found one daughter among the three who was a loving child, and in the end right triumphs. Goneril and Regan are defeated, retribution falls upon them, Lear is restored to his throne, and Cordelia succeeds him as Queen. So the old play tells the story, and so Spenser tells it again in *The Faerie Queene*. But as Shakespeare concludes his play he seems to be deliberately depriving it of all poetic justice and of all apparent moral significance. The loving daughter is involved in the general disaster of the House of Lear, against all authority of history or stage. So also in the parallel sub-plot of Gloucester and his sons, introduced from Sidney's *Arcadia*, the happy ending of Sidney's story is changed to tragedy. In the end, the storm of untoward events, reflected in the thunder and lightning and great wind of the conflicting elements, passes. There remains, said Coleridge, 'the closing in of night, and the single hope of darkness.'

A considerable chorus of comment has chimed in with this grievous verdict upon the greatest of tragedies. Robert Bridges tells us that if Shakespeare's object in *Othello* is to excite his audience, in *Macbeth* to terrify it, and in *Hamlet* to mystify it, in *King Lear* his object is to harrow it. For Miss Lena Ashwell, a great Shakespearean actress of this century, as for Tolstoy also, the play is a dead march of pessimism. 'We find Greek pessimism in *Lear*,' she wrote.[1] Ruskin's complaint is that we do not find Greek optimism in *Lear*. The enemy in Shakespeare is blind fate, as Miss Ashwell also complained. The fault of haste or indiscretion brings results terrible beyond all bounds.

> At the close of a Shakespeare tragedy, nothing remains but dead march and clothes of burial. At the close of a Greek tragedy there are far-off sounds of a divine triumph, and a glory as of resurrection.[2]

It is perhaps odd that Aristotle did not feel this in Greek tragedy, or at any rate did not express this feeling. But we may well hold that this is precisely what we feel in *King Lear*, if not in Greek tragedy.

The only philosophy that can possibly see in *King Lear* the mere fall of black night upon a shipwreck of human life and love is materialism, which encloses life within final limits of time and space. In such a view a famous couplet of Pope might well express the cosmic significance of the play.

> Thy hand, great Anarch, let the curtain fall
> And universal darkness cover all.

But indeed the truth would be more disastrous. For such a philosophy the world has neither Ruler nor Anarch, neither order nor monarchy, neither God nor Devil in command, but is a ship not only without a compass or a captain, but without a sea.

1. *Reflections upon Shakespeare* (1927).
2. *Modern Painters* ix II. 15.

Much play has been made of the setting of *King Lear* in a pagan world of pre-Christian Britain, and of Shakespeare's possible exclusion of Christian thought from its moral and spiritual atmosphere.[1] This has led to interpretations of the play as resting upon a stoic philosophy, along with a materialistic view of life and of the universe, though these are inconsistent one with another, and are also remote from the truth. Certainly the stoic attitude towards life preserves the invulnerability of the virtuous philosopher, who may justly take refuge in suicide, in contempt for the incalculable, uncontrolled circumstance that destroys him. But of this, whatever we may find in *Julius Caesar,* there is nothing in *King Lear.* Lear himself is certainly the least invulnerable of men, and furthest of all from the Senecal man of Chapman's admiration. Othello does not take refuge in death, he executes justice upon himself, well aware that this act does not close his account. Hamlet considers the stoic solution, only to reject it. Iago comes nearest to stoic self-sufficiency, disdainful of the final disastrous throw of the dice, silent and impassive. Gloucester sets aside the temptation, as Hamlet does:

> You ever gentle gods,
> Let not my worser spirit tempt me again
> To die before you please.

Nor does Edmund fall into this pit, though there was excuse for him. It is worth noting that Shakespeare reduces the guilt of the Edmund whom he took from the *Arcadia*. There it is Edmund himself who with re-

---

1. It has not, however, been sufficiently observed that it is a deliberate variation from the old play of *Leir,* in which we have a Christian world, with a Saviour, a Church, and even an accusation of Puritanism levelled at Cordelia.

volting cruelty tears out his father's old eyes. In Shakespeare he is not even present when Cornwall, before Regan's eyes, does the hideous deed. But he is born to contempt in the society in which he is an unwelcome intruder, even to his father, for whom he is the visible memory of his 'pleasant vices,' as Edgar put it. For Albany, he is 'half-blooded fellow.' He stands from his very birth 'in the plague of custom,' bastard and base-born. And yet in the end of all, he seeks to make amends. 'Some good I mean to do,' and dies true brother to Edgar after all, and no brother to Iago.

There is in fact poetic justice enough in *King Lear*. Goneril, Regan, Cornwall and Edmund, all perish in their sins. Evil is destroyed. Towards the end of the play Albany proclaims the restoration of the old King to his absolute power, and of Edgar and Kent to their just rights:

> All friends shall taste
> The wages of their virtue, and all foes
> The cup of their deservings.

But poetic justice seems to be of little moment. When Edmund's death is reported to Albany, he truly comments, 'that's but a trifle here,' as indeed it is. When the news of the desperate deaths of Goneril and Regan comes to Lear, he puts it aside carelessly as an irrelevance, 'Ay, so I think.' And hard upon Albany's proclamation, to which the old king pays no attention, it is cancelled by Lear's death. As for Kent, restored to his rights, and more, he has a journey shortly to go, to join his master. Albany's justice beats the air. Of what avail indeed would it be to set Lear and Cordelia, Gloucester and Kent, afloat again in that 'ebb and flow of great ones' that Lear mocks so gently, but so irrevocably.

The truth is that greater issues are afoot in this play than the verdicts of justice or the nice balance of rights and wrongs in the universe. We have long ago learned to recognise in its action and development a theme which might justify the title *The Redemption of King Lear* in place of *The Tragedy of King Lear*, pointing to a happy ending of deeper truth than Tate's or that desired by Bradley. It is a theme that recurs elsewhere in Shakespeare, in comedy as in tragedy. It is something of a key to the significance of *The Taming of the Shrew,* in which Katherine finds her true self and with it happiness. In *Troilus and Cressida* again, Troilus, lost in love, perplexed and frustrated by Cressida's weak disloyalty, comes at last to his full manhood as a Prince of Troy at war against her enemies, pursuing duty instead of his own private ends, and goes forth to certain death in battle with the mantle of dead Hector upon him. So with Lear who has hitherto, as Goneril justly says, but slenderly known himself, and comes to fuller knowledge and with it a deeper understanding of the world of men and of their universe, through the desperate evils let loose by his own act. From overweening pride, security, and obstinacy, he moves through rebellious anger, despair, and madness to patience, to humility, and to a new recognition of truth and goodness. In the great storm of events he suffers a sea-change, purged by suffering. Much has been made, as by Bradley and later critics, of the apparent paradox of Lear's passivity throughout the movement of the play, though he is its principal character, as if he were something like a soul in purgatory. But his activity is within the microcosmos of his own conscious being, and it is intense. Deep within the very core of this activity lies the problem of justice, that justice which in the catastrophe of the play appears to be contemned and almost irrelevant.

In Shakespeare's later plays the question of the operation of justice comes constantly into dramatic consideration, which vividly reflects the poet's deep concern with the problem. In *Measure for Measure* the whole action rests upon an image of the delegation of the powers of justice from God to Kings, as trustees for divine justice. So the Duke vests his royal powers in his deputy Angelo, and is content to observe unseen. The tyranny of formal laws, the fallibility of their human instrument, and their corruption and abuse in practice, lead to the Duke's intervention and to his resumption of his supreme function so that right may be done. In the bankruptcy of justice, mercy and charity make amends, extended even to the corrupt justicer. It is difficult to refrain from pursuing the image further, into the robe of religion worn by the Duke, a symbol of his divine function, into the noviceship of Isabella whose plea is throughout for mercy, and into the marriage of justice and mercy in their persons with which the play concludes.

In *The Tempest* we have a rightful Duke in exile upon an island where he is sole master, determining events and controlling destinies, inflicting punishment and showing mercy, with spirits at his call and with the elements in his command as instruments of his will. His power is supernatural, and is wielded by himself in his absolute decision. The law and the justice of

Prospero upon his island reflect in its limited sphere something closely akin to a world controlled by a constant and sufficient intervention of divine justice in direct operation upon human destinies and actions, by a law of visitations, in the Elizabethan sense of the word. He is capable of anger at evil, like the wrath of God. He puts men's hearts to test. There is mercy and forgiveness for penitence in the evildoer, in which Caliban also has his share. So the island which Gonzalo would govern in all the simplicity and beauty of the golden age has also a form of justice that is utopian, and yet rules the universe. In the world of men it is indeed utopian. When Prospero returns from his island to that world, to his Dukedom and to Milan, he breaks his staff, buries his book, and abdicates those powers that surpass royal power.

These two plays are comedies, and in them the dramatic treatment of the question of justice is not incompatible with a mind that is merely curious in its analysis of the operation of justice in human life. In the tragedies of *Macbeth, Othello,* and *Hamlet,* specific problems of justice are met, and solved. But in *King Lear* it may well seem that that analysis has become destructive, that a logical dilemma has moved into a philosophic quandary, that the function of justice itself has come into question, a devastating thought. It is, of course, a familiar thought in the Christian world. 'Though thou slay me, yet will I trust in thee.' But this trust rests upon the admission of ignorance of the evidence, and upon a faith overcoming individual judgment. It is another doubt altogether that questions the validity of the principle and its significance in human life.

When this tragedy opens, Lear himself, like the Emperor Valentinian in Fletcher's play, *is* justice and wields that power by virtue of his kingship. The very first scene in the play shows that power in direct action, even as Stuart London from time to time saw King James sitting himself, as he was entitled to do, on the Bench of his Court of Star Chamber. Lear is engaged upon one of the two main limbs of justice as it appeared to Aristotle and as it appears also to our modern world, Distributive Justice and Retributive Justice. In the modern world we are accustomed to Distributive Justice, the lean kine, swallowing up the once fat kine of Retributive Justice. And we are becoming gradually less inclined to consent even in works of imagination to the operation of justice as retributive. King Lear, surprisingly, is exercising distributive justice from the throne, though he rests his judgment upon merit, contrary to the enlightened modern view of social justice. Goneril and Regan satisfy the claims of merit, as Lear has formulated it, but against all his expectation Cordelia fails the test, and retributive justice also comes at once into action, upon an ungrateful daughter and a rebellious servant Kent, Lear nothing doubting his right to exercise it nor questioning his own decision. Yet he is not by nature tyrannical or unjust or given to hatred. From these decrees the dread train of events flows inevitably, in which Lear's whole world suddenly gives way under his feet. The idea upon which the play rests is indeed the consequence of a grave error and abuse of justice by the king within whose powers justice lies.

As the action develops, Lear himself is led to consider power more closely, and with it justice, the sword of power. Here Shakespeare makes a significant change in the story of Lear as Holinshed tells it. In Holinshed, Lear retains the half of his royal estate, and retains his throne, content to give great rewards to his daughters and to assure to them the succession to all. But in Shakespeare he gives all at once, and his crown too, and with it he abdicates also from his power to dispense justice, and becomes subject to justice for the first time. No longer a king, no longer hedged about with divinity, a mere 'idle old man,' as Goneril puts it scornfully, he is the better able now to examine kingship, the sanctions of royal power, and justice, with eyes no longer veiled by their exercise in his own person. 'I think the King is but a man,' says Shakespeare's Henry the Fifth, and philosophises a good deal upon the theme. But it is all very theoretical, such an essay as that absolute monarch Henry the Eighth might have written for his tutor. But heaven help the tutor if the essay were not applauded with an *alpha plus*. King Hal's essay is something like a report of a Royal Commission of one, signed *Henry R*.

> No, thou proud dream,
> I am a king that find thee, and I know.

It is vastly different with Lear.

> I *was* a king that find thee, and I know.

> When the rain came to wet me once, and the wind to make me chatter; when the thunder would not peace at my bidding; there I found 'em, there I smelt 'em out. Go to, they are not men o' their words; they told me I was everything. 'Tis a lie, I am not ague-proof.

As the play opens with the King doing justice, so other, briefer, trial-scenes comment further upon power and justice. The mad parody of a trial in Act III. Sc. 6 is prefaced by the Fool's searching question:

> Prithe nuncle tell me, whether a madman be a gentleman or a yeoman,

to which Lear replies, 'A king, a king.' The Justices in this trial are madmen too, save one. There are three, Edgar as Poor Tom, the Fool, and Kent added to the Bench as an afterthought. Lear is the accuser, and he too is mad. The honourable assembly of judges sitting upon his cause is a crazy phantasmagoria that shifts and dissolves into nothingness. The scene is followed hot-foot by Cornwall's brief trial of Gloucester. He has scruples not concerning justice, but concerning the forms of justice, which forbid the execution of Gloucester. Yet he diverts justice to the vengeance of wrath served by mere power beyond men's control, in the execution of Gloucester's eyes. And in this doing of injustice the false justicer himself meets his death-wound at the hands of one of his servants, of one of those whose control he mocks. Such is the exercise of power, the master of justice.

In the next act we have further scathing analysis of justice in action:

> See how yond justice rails upon yond simple thief.
> Hark in thine ear. Change places; and handy-dandy, which is the justice, which is the thief?

Gloucester, like justice, is blind, yet may well see how the world goes, with no eyes. A farmer's dog barking at a beggar is 'the great image of authority — a dog's obeyed in office.' The dispensers and the instruments of justice are corrupt and evil themselves. Plaintiff and defendant alike are but guilty in different ways. And justice is merely impotent. The kingship itself is not left unscathed in Lear's sharp irony: 'No, they cannot touch me for coining; I am the King himself.'

Finally, there is the great storm and wind, the heavens and earth at war. In the old play the storm stands for divine anger. The thunder and lightning are the signs of the coming intervention of Jupiter, of divine justice. But in Shakespeare, deliberately and plainly, this is changed into a reflection of disorder and chaos, the elements in hideous battle, driven into strife at the will of the purposeless, violent gods above, as if the universe were distraught. And this is what breaks Lear's already precarious sanity. It is the ultimate doubt concerning justice, that even in the heavens there is no certainty or security. Power and justice are weighed in the balance—the vaunted image of dispassionate justice—and are found wanting.

When we think of this appalling analysis of justice, we may well wonder why so much comment has been concentrated upon Lear's outburst against luxury and lechery, as if that were the core and heart of his revolt of the spirit, as if it were an explosion of Shakespeare's own personal revolt against sex, of his utter disillusionment. But in comparison this is formal, commonplace, trite, and insignificant.

How are we then to think of the complex, profound re-birth of the spirit in Lear out of these depths that he has plumbed, and out of which he emerges into a new light? Is the true subject and conclusion of this tremendous play the purging of Lear through suffering, an *exemplum* of the theological concept of the Problem of Pain? It has even been put that Lear's

Purgatory is here and now in this world, not in the world to come, though Purgatory is peopled only by souls already redeemed. It would be gravely disturbing to the spirit if this were indeed the final teaching of the play, the true interpretation of its action as Shakespeare conceived and created it. If the world of Lear was truly purgatorial in this sense, then Lear's concern was for his own salvation. Having been subjected to a deep educative process, he submits to it and accepts it, so that he may pass an all-important examination. The gods do not after all kill us for their sport; they only kill us for our own good, a far more desperate conclusion. But it is indeed not so in *King Lear*.

When the tide turns and the light begins to shine again upon Lear's troubled being, it is not of himself that he is thinking, not even of his immortal soul. 'In boy, go first,' he says to the shivering Fool—out of the bitter storm into the poor shelter of the hovel.

> Nay get thee in. I'll pray, and then I'll sleep.
> Poor naked wretches, wheresoe'er you are
> That bide the pelting of this pitiless storm,
> How shall your houseless heads, and unfed sides,
> Your looped and windowed raggedness, defend you
> From seasons such as this? O I have ta'en
> Too little care of this.

So Gloucester too, to his son Edgar, poor Tom:

> In fellow there, into the hovel; keep thee warm.

The Christian concept of charity is sweeping like a great tide into his soul, as into Gloucester's, the tide in which Cordelia and Kent have ever floated as in their own native element. In such an element forgiveness becomes a superfluity, an irrelevance:

> *Lear:* I know you do not love me, for your sisters
> Have, as I remember, done me wrong.
> You have some cause, they have not.
>
> *Cor:* No cause, no cause.

Love casteth out doubt also. We recall two kneelings of Lear to daughters. He kneels before Regan in Act II. Sc. 4. There he kneels in outraged satire, in parody of submission, an 'unsightly trick' as Regan calls it at once. In Act V he is about to kneel to Cordelia:

> When thou dost ask my blessing, I'll kneel down,
> And ask of *thee* forgiveness.

'No cause, no cause.' If there is a truly theological basis for this play, it is that evil is to be known and feared because it is the absence of good, that hatred is dreadful because it arises out of the absence of love. The end of the play is surely the triumph of love, of positive goodness.

Edgar reveals himself to Gloucester, and asks his blessing. And Gloucester, overcome by this revelation of unshakeable love, torn between joy and grief, dies in ecstasy. 'His flawed heart . . . burst smilingly.' Kent asks no reward for the steadfast loyalty of his love for Lear. That love is beyond reason or purpose.

> I have a journey, sir, shortly to go.
> My master calls me, I must not say no.

Love, as Shakespeare had written before he wrote *King Lear*,

> Love is not love,
> Which alters when it alteration finds ...
> O no, it is an ever fixed mark
> That looks on tempests and is never shaken.

Cordelia's husband, the King of France, echoes these words early in this play:

> Love's not love
> When it is mingled with regards that stand
> Aloof from the entire point.

Beyond the facile satisfaction of an old fairy tale, beyond the defiance of a Prometheus or the stoic fortitude of Eteocles in Greek tragedy, beyond the stony anaesthesia of Shelley's Beatrice Cenci, 'all fear and pain being subdued,' is the reconciliation in *King Lear* that comes despite the evil of the world, the apparent injustice of fate impartial in its destruction of good and evil alike, in the fulfilment of a soul's destiny — that too, not in 'calm of mind, all passion spent,' as with Milton's Samson, but shaken still by mortality, as Christ was in the Garden of Gethsemane.

So we are led back to the deep criticism of power and justice upon which this play has so much to say. It has but little to say upon divine justice in direct intervention or indirect, though this was so familiar and accepted a feature of the Elizabethan moral landscape. And what it says is all incidental, and contradictory. The gods are just, and use our vices to plague us, says Edgar, yet Gloucester accuses these gods whom elsewhere he calls 'kind,' and 'ever-gentle,' of slaying men for their wanton sport. Lear himself invokes the judgment of Heaven and the just cause of the goddess Nature, yet considers whether the gods themselves have not set his daughters upon him to plague him. Both are at one with Eteocles in the *Seven against Thebes* in their dark moments. 'The only favour the gods enjoy from us is our death,' he complains, and he dies submissive to impotence against the evils sent down upon man by the gods. But praise and blame of the gods alternate in *King Lear* and are little more than expletives. Only Albany speaks in terms of conviction of a judgment of the heavens that falls upon Goneril and Regan. It seems to be the true conclusion of *King Lear* that power and justice, human or divine, are none of them ultimately important after all.

There are crucial phrases in the four tragedies that are the more significant here because the word 'cause' is so deeply coloured in Elizabethan use by its judicial associations. 'It is the cause, it is the cause,' says Othello. 'All causes must give way,' says Macbeth. 'Report me and my cause aright,' says Hamlet to Horatio. 'No cause, no cause,' says Cordelia in pure love. And so in the universe, in God's love for man, and man's love for God, and man's love for man, if we did but understand it. The concepts of the less or more, the fine balance of right and wrong, even the most well meant of human attempts to reflect the divine assessment of God's creatures, all are mortal, and fallible. And when we know this, and come to live by this knowledge, then we are at one with the true power and with the ultimate justice that reigns causeless in the universe, with 'the love that moves the sun and all the stars,' the shining vision that is the supreme bliss of eternal life.

APPENDIX ON HAMLET

Note A. Laertes

i. Act IV, Sc. 7. 1.58. 'Thus didst thou.'

The character of Laertes and his function are deeply involved in the problem of justice which underlies the action of the play. Like Hamlet, he too finds it laid upon him to right a grievous wrong and to become an instrument of justice. His situation after the slaying of his father Polonius by Hamlet is a close parallel to that of Hamlet himself, and the twin dramatic studies of these two young men confronting their duty form one of the principal sources of interest in this rich play.

It has recently been proposed to emend 'Thus didst thou' to 'Thus diest thou' in Act IV, Sc. 7.[1] The emendation is more momentous than would appear in the arguments, for it involves deep significances in the action and in the character of Laertes. Plausible at first sight, it may appeal to actors and producers concerned with the part. But it is far from innocuous.

The basic authoritative texts of *Hamlet*, the Second Quarto and the First Folio, offer no support for this emendation. But the pirated First Quarto of 1603 is cited as reading:

That I shall live to tell him, thus he dies,

and as giving evidence that 'diest' must have been at some stage in the promptbook. The assumption here is that the compositor of Q.2 misread Shakespeare's

1. H. Jenkins, in *Modern Language Review.* LIV. pp. 391-5.

[99]

copy, and that a corrupt edition preserves some reflection of the manuscript reading and of the words actually spoken on the stage. Few indeed will be found to award decisive authority to Q.1 as against a reading in Q.2 and F.1 which offers no difficulty. There is good reason for believing the readings of these two authoritative editions to have been independent here, the one from Shakespeare's own manuscript, the other from the prompt-copy prepared for the stage. We must therefore assume that two compositors were guilty of the same misreading of their copy.

The graphic argument in its simplest form, that the letters *d* and *e* are readily confused in the secretary hand which Shakespeare wrote, is of course plausible enough. But it may be pressed too far. I have had the curiosity to examine a large number of examples of the sequence *est* in a wide variety of secretary hands. None offered the possibility of confusion. Patterns of groups of letters are important in the use of graphic arguments for textual purposes.

But critical considerations are more cogent still. It is no mere question of 'so feeble a taunt'[1] contained in the words 'Thus didst thou,' as compared with the more dramatic 'Thus diest thou,' as is argued for the emendation. It is in fact a deadly accusation. Laertes is concerned to avenge his father's death as an act of justice as well as of revenge, which is 'wild justice.' Faced with the general rumour, of which Claudius is well aware, that the slayer was Claudius, Laertes faces also the deadly prospect of killing the King, breaking his allegiance and risking the damnation inherent in regicide, despite the 'divinity that doth hedge a King,'

1. Ibid. p. 394.

as Claudius has just said. Claudius knows his danger. And Gertrude is quick to come to his rescue. Polonius is dead, 'but not by him' is her immediate ejaculation to Laertes. The peace of mind and satisfaction that Laertes seeks can only come from the doing of justice upon his father's slayer, and this he will do at all cost to himself, as a filial duty and in all honour. Satisfied in due course that not the King, but Hamlet, is the slayer, upon his second interview with Claudius he first demands why the King did not execute justice himself, but presently agrees to collaborate with him as the instrument of their joint destruction of Hamlet. Under the King's malign influence the agreement gradually changes from the fair duel, fit for an honourable man and compatible with Laertes' swordsmanship, to a conspiracy to ensure Hamlet's death. But this comes at the end of the interview. A fair fight is still in Laertes' mind when he speaks the words with which we are concerned, before his honour has been smirched by Claudius. He will do justice upon Hamlet, and will let justice be seen to be done, by Hamlet as by others, in the doing. He will accuse Hamlet 'to his teeth,' face to face. He will thrust at him—and his gesture makes this plain here—with the words 'Thus didst thou,' to my father when you slew him, and thus I justly avenge that slaying. 'Thus diest thou' are the words of a mere gangster killer. 'Thus didst thou' are the words of an instrument of vengeful justice.

Laertes' essential preoccupation with justice and honour emerges plainly at the end of the subsequent sword-play: 'And yet it is almost against my conscience,' and again: 'I am justly killed with mine own treachery,' The King too 'is justly served.' And with

APPENDIX [101]

his last words Laertes absolves Hamlet from all claims for justice and revenge. Shakespeare's triumph lies in the transformation of a crude story of revenge and in the creation of characters far removed from the lay-figures of mere vengefulness. Of these, Laertes is not the least subtle and memorable, nor are these three crucial words the least significant.

ii. *Act IV. Sc.5.*[1]

It is only a misunderstanding of the essential stage-business of this busy scene that can create difficulties in the original texts. It is a mere quibble to object to 'Danes' as an interpretation of the 'others' who in Q.2 accompany Laertes breaking through the King's guarded door. Gertrude describes them as 'you false Danish dogs' immediately before their entrance. It is quite clear that in Q.2 they enter with Laertes and stay back-stage while he advances. There is then a brief dialogue between them and Laertes, the result of which is that they leave him, upon his orders, and stay outside to guard the door. It is difficult to argue that this dialogue is carried on between Laertes on stage and 'others' off stage, on the mere ground that F. reads 'Enter Laertes' and not 'Enter Laertes with others.' F., like Q.2, has the dialogue between Laertes and 'All.' and 'No let's come in,' spoken from back-stage, presents no difficulty. They stand inside the door, awaiting orders. 'Let's come in' does not of necessity mean 'Let's come on stage.' It is plain that upon their exit they are posted outside of the door, for Laertes commands them so. 'I thank you, keep the door.' He is himself in danger, and needs their continued presence within call.

1. Ibid.

The next event is the arrival of Ophelia seeking entrance. It is announced by a further 'noise within,' from which emerges naturally enough the decision of the guards to let her through, and hence the cry 'within,' 'Let her come in.' She is no enemy, but Laertes' sister. The 'noise within' does not consist of the words 'Let her come in,' but is a commotion preceding them. As for attributing these words to Claudius as an order on the ground that he is the most important person present, the fact is that Claudius is not in command. His Switzers have been broken and have fled. He has no power over Laertes' guards at the door. And there is no evidence that either Claudius or Laertes knew that it was Ophelia until she was actually let through the door and on stage. Neither could speak these words. Ophelia's first entrance earlier in the scene is a very different affair. Gertrude and the Gentleman and Horatio are discussing Ophelia. Gertrude begins by saying 'I will not speak with her,' and none but she could possibly give the order 'Let her come in.' The situations are not analogous, though the words are coincidental.

The bibliographical facts offer no difficulty. There are instances enough of the confusion by a compositor of stage-direction with dialogue, as here in Q.2. F. remedies this confusion. We cannot put aside its reading here, while accepting as authoritative its reading against Q.2 of 'Enter Laertes' against 'Enter Laertes with others,' merely in the interests of a proposed emendation which does not improve upon the accepted version of these events, and indeed would make less good 'theatre' of the scene.

Note B. Hamlet

Act IV, Sc.4, 11.173-5.

heaven hath pleased it so
To punish me with this, and this with me,
That I must be their scourge and minister.

These difficult lines have received the close attention of commentators, with surprising conclusions as to their meaning. It seems to be agreed that what it has pleased Heaven to do is to punish Hamlet for his slaying of Polonius, and to punish Polonius by the instrumentality of Hamlet. In this interpretation Hamlet foresees at once his punishment in the revelation of his secret intentions to Claudius, who will realise that Hamlet killed Polonius by mistake for himself, and will therefore have good reason for planning to kill Hamlet. But it is evident that the slaying of Polonius makes no difference to Claudius' appreciation of Hamlet's intention, nor to his handling of the situation. The Play scene had already made the situation abundantly clear on both sides. It was war to the knife. And Claudius had already, as a direct result of the Play scene, arranged for the killing of Hamlet on his arrival in England, as rightly observed in a recent closely reasoned discussion of the passage.[1]

It is therefore far from clear wherein lies the punishment of Hamlet in fact. Nor is it clear, one may add, for what sin or crime against Heaven Polonius is punished by Heaven through Hamlet's action. It is hardly enough that he was, in Hamlet's phrase, a 'rash, intruding fool.' And certainly there is no evidence of

---

[1]. F. Bowers, in *Publications of the Modern Language Association.* Sept. 1955, pp. 740-9.

his complicity in the crimes of Claudius, as there is none concerning Gertrude. As for Hamlet, Professor Bowers concludes that the punishment of Hamlet is due to his unjustified murder of Polonius, as generally agreed, his guilt and disobedience requiring the penalty of death. This exegesis is further expounded in the phrase 'their scourge and minister.' By virtue of his guilt, Hamlet may be a 'scourge' used by Heaven for its own ends, as often a man damned for his sins was used, as was Tamburlaine, to punish erring mankind. But he may equally be a 'minister' of God's anger under the commands of Heaven transmitted by the Ghost. This, the argument proceeds, is Hamlet's dilemma from the beginning, whether to pursue at once his private revenge as a 'scourge' or to await obediently the sign that the appointed hour for action as a 'minister' and public avenger has struck, with a preordained opportunity for that action, which will be guiltless and without danger to himself. This doubt in Hamlet's mind explains his depressed self-examination and his delays. He resists the temptation to act in the Prayer scene, but obeys an impulse, no longer awaiting the sign from Heaven, when he kills Polonius in error for Claudius. Thus, it is concluded, Heaven foreseeing his action, punishes him in the present by allowing an innocent victim to fall to his sword, and in the future by allowing his own fall, the fall of a guilty man, to murderous plots. It is a very complex and thorny exegesis, resting upon narrow theological implications in the terms 'scourge' and 'minister' and upon fine distinctions between prescience and predestination.

But indeed it raises more difficulties than it solves. It assumes that Heaven's direction of events would contemplate the shedding of innocent blood as part of its plan. It equates Hamlet with notorious 'scourges,' atheists like Tamburlaine and Attila. If Hamlet is a 'scourge,' a sinner damned for his sins, the concluding invocation by Horatio of flights of angels to sing him to his rest, made beyond question with general approval, becomes meaningless. Hamlet's phrase, be it observed, is 'scourge *and* minister,' and in his mind the two are clearly not incompatible. Indeed, to Hamlet's mind, it is in his capacity as a minister of Heaven that he becomes involved in action as a scourge or punisher of evil, and so the audience would take the matter. The audience has long since understood Hamlet's function, from his first tormented appreciation of the task that appears to have been laid upon him, after the revelations of the Ghost. There is evil abroad in Denmark, and it is his unhappy fate to have been 'born to set it right.' The 'cursed spite' of such a fate, then already felt by Hamlet, is close indeed to this later concept that the imposition by Heaven of the task of being its scourge and minister is a punishment in itself. It has pleased Heaven to lay this burden upon him, and to punish through him the evil abroad in Denmark: 'To punish me with this, and this with me.' There is august authority for such an approach to the will of Heaven, for Christ himself prayed that the cup might be taken from him. The significance of these lines has been blurred by the desire to relate them immediately to the death of Polonius.